8 Myths that keep Christians
SINGLE

Dr. Denver Cheddie

Indira Rampaul-Cheddie

I Kissed Waiting Goodbye: 8 Myths that Keep Christians SINGLE

Copyright © 2018 by Denver Cheddie and Indira Rampaul-Cheddie
All rights reserved. With the exception of the use of brief quotations, no portion of this book may be reproduced or used in any manner whatsoever without the express written permission of the authors.

Copyright registered with the US Library of Congress

ISBN-13: 978-1721137503
ISBN-10: 1721137505

8myths.com

Unless otherwise stated, all scripture citations are taken from the NEW KING JAMES VERSION®, NKJV. Copyright© 1982 by Thomas Nelson, Inc. Used by permission. All rights reserved.

Scriptures marked KJV are taken from the KING JAMES VERSION (KJV), public domain.

Scriptures marked NIV are taken from the Holy Bible, New International Version®, NIV®. Copyright © 1973, 1978, 1984, 2011 by Biblica, Inc.™ Used by permission of Zondervan. All rights reserved worldwide. www.zondervan.com The *"NIV"* and *"New International Version"* are trademarks registered in the United States Patent and Trademark Office by Biblica, Inc.™

Cover photo courtesy Pixabay. Used with permission.

This book presents testimonies and experiences of individuals with their permission. In some cases, names have been changed and details slightly modified without altering the gist of their stories.

Disponible en Español – busca *"Besé esperando el adios"* en Amazon

Denver and Indira wish to
dedicate this book to each other

God blessed the broken road

that led me straight to you

TABLE OF CONTENTS

PREFACE	1
ARE MYTHS KEEPING YOU SINGLE?	2
MYTH #1 Waiting for "the one" that God created just for you	10
MYTH #2 Waiting for "God's perfect will in God's perfect timing"	22
MYTH #3 Waiting to "hear from God" first	37
MYTH #4 Waiting for God to "work it out"	54
MYTH #5 Over-complicating it	72
MYTH #6 Being too fussy	86
MYTH #7 Not being fussy enough	98
MYTH #8 Misunderstanding the role of parents	113
YOUR ACTION PLAN	123
ABOUT THE AUTHORS	128

PREFACE

Would you like to go down in history as the greatest unmarried Christian of all time? Or would you just prefer to find a husband or wife?

That's exactly what I thought. You are not trying to break any Guinness World Record. You are not trying to maximize your singlehood (as if there is even such a thing). You are just trying to get married and live happily ever after. So why are there so many books for single Christian out there teaching them everything other than how to actually find a husband or wife?

While doing research for this book, we looked at a number of other popular books for single Christians. Christians are taught to kiss dating goodbye and to savor their singleness as they wait patiently for their Boaz. There are also tons of devotionals for single Christians.

All of these things have their place in your Christian walk. But they are not designed to help you in your search for Mr. Right or Ms. Right. They are designed to fill you with hope (which is great), positive emotions (which are great), resolve (also great), and to teach you how to occupy yourself while single (again great). But they don't provide you with SCRIPTURAL GUIDANCE to help you in your search.

That's where *I Kissed Waiting Goodbye* comes in. We provide single Christians with scriptural guidance to help you in your search for a husband or wife. This book will fill you with hope, strength and resolve. You will experience the rollercoaster ride of emotions, the adrenalin rush, and all that jazz. But most of all, we provide guidance – and it's all from the Bible. What should I do? What should I not do? What should I stop doing? How do I maximize my prospects of finding a good husband or wife?

We also debunk a lot of the misguidance you might have had. There are a lot of misinterpretations of scripture that cause single Christians to go about their search in the wrong way. They simply do not work, as you may already have figured out. These teachings cause Christians to remain single longer than they need to.

As we open up the scriptures, we pray that God's Word will truly come alive in your life, and will illuminate your way forward. We pray that God's Word will truly be a light unto your path to guide you in your journey from singleness to marriage.

ARE MYTHS KEEPING YOU SINGLE?

What was Whitney waiting for?

Whitney served as the youth leader in her local church. Whitney was beautiful. She had a great job, she loved the Lord and was committed to serving Him with all her heart and soul. But Whitney was single. Into her late 20s, Whitney still did not find what she was looking for. There weren't a lot of Christian men in her church, and Whitney did not visit other churches. Instead she believed that God would send *"the one"* to find her.

Very quickly she found herself in her 30s. All her friends were getting married. Some of the women whom Whitney had mentored while serving as their youth leader – even they were getting married. But Whitney was still waiting for *"the one."* Everyone else in the church looked on with amazement. How could someone that beautiful and that outstanding as a Christian woman still be single? They reasoned among themselves, *"I guess for someone that special, God has to have a really great guy in store."* They comforted themselves by saying this was why it was taking so long.

On one occasion, a visiting pastor spoke at one of their youth meetings. He proceeded to lambast the single men of the church. How could they see a single woman so beautiful and not scoop her up? He called up Whitney and *"prophesied"* to her that in one year, God would bring the Christian man that He had appointed for her. You know the story. One year came and went, and nothing happened. *"The one"* remained a no-show. Many other years came and went, but Whitney never met *"the one."*

There were a couple of guys who tried to ask Whitney out. But each time, they received a very hostile rejection. They walked away humiliated as if they had committed some horrible sin. But they eventually moved on and married other women. Whitney remained single. One guy, who was married and had no romantic interest in Whitney, saw her at work one day and attempted to say a polite hello. He too received a rather snobbish response. Did Whitney hate men, or was she just clueless as to how things were supposed to work?

Soon Whitney was in her 40s. With her entire youth now behind her, the chances of her ever getting married seemed less and less likely. She had long outgrown the youth group. People started saying that her best chance of getting married was if a pastor's wife died and he took Whitney as his second wife. But not even this happened. Whitney remains single to this day.

Where did it go wrong for Whitney? Why couldn't she get married in her 20s, have a family and live happily ever after? Why did someone so outstanding have to remain single all her life? Did God hate her? Was Whitney just unlucky? Was it just never meant to be? Could it be that there was simply nobody good enough for her? Was it God's will for her to remain single? Did God have some really special purpose that required Whitney to remain single?

The real reason Whitney remained single is because Whitney believed in myths. She was not single because of the shortage of men in the church. Yes there was a shortage of men in her church, but other women were getting married. Whitney was single because she believed things that were simply not true. She waited patiently for things God never promised. She was taught myths regarding how to go about finding a husband. She convinced herself of things that were false. Whitney could have got married very early. But she insisted that she wait for *"the one."* She was waiting for God, not realizing that God was waiting for her.

You will hear the occasional testimony of someone who waited patiently for *"the one"*, and in the *"fullness of time"* God worked it out *"miraculously."* But for every one of those testimonies with a positive ending, there are a dozen others who wait in vain and never find *"the one."* In fact just recently, one guy wrote me lamenting that from age 19, he was taught to *"wait for God to send him a wife."* Today he is 53 and still single.

These stories make me sad and angry at the same time. God never told us to wait for *"the one."* That is a myth that is keeping Christians single longer than they need to be.

Kody kissed dating goodbye

Kody was in his 30s. He was a devout Christian and he was looking for *"the one"* as well. Who exactly is this *"one"* everybody is waiting for? And how many *"ones"* are there?

After years of frustration, Kody wrote me through my website and asked for my counsel. He never had a girlfriend and never dated. But he was very much interested in getting married. However, he did not believe in dating. Perhaps he had read Joshua Harris' book.

I questioned him why he did not want to date. He believed that dating would be like cheating on his future wife. *"Even if you don't have sex?"* I asked him. He insisted that even if they didn't have sex, it would still be cheating. *"So how would you ever meet 'the one' if you don't date?"* Kody was not sure. Supposedly, God would bring this person into Kody's life while he occupied himself with the work of the Lord. Here is what I told Kody.

> *Let's break it down. You can't get married unless you meet "the one." You can't meet "the one" unless you do some form of dating. But you won't date because if you date someone other than "the one", that would be like cheating on "the one." Essentially you won't date until you meet "the one", and you won't meet "the one" unless you date. Your mind is in a standoff with itself.*
>
> *The next question to ask is, how do you know who "the one" is if you don't date the person? Other than getting to know people socially (which is essentially what Christian dating is), the only other way you can know if someone is "the one" is if God tells you.*
>
> *Of course, God knows the future. But you have trapped yourself in a vicious cycle where unless God tells you who "the one" is, you will remain single all your life. That's not a good place to be. The Bible never teaches that you need a revelation from God to get married. You just need to get rid of those misguided beliefs (myths) that are keeping you single. This is a classic example of how believing myths – that are not found anywhere in God's Word – can keep you single longer than you need to be.*

Again, you will hear testimonies from people who claimed that God spoke to them about their future husband or wife, and things worked out exactly as God said. But for every such testimony, there are at least a dozen others who thought they heard from God only to realize later in life, how horribly wrong they were. God gives us guidance as well as wisdom.

It is not easy being a single Christian

Whitney and Kody depict the experiences and the struggles of many single Christian men and women today. They are devout Christians, they love the Lord and they genuinely want to meet *"the one"* and get married. They look at others who effortlessly find a mate and get married young, yet they have to struggle and fight. They question God, they argue with God, they threaten to backslide. It is so unfair. How could God say He is no favorer of persons?

They have read all the Christian books out there for singles. They have kissed dating goodbye. They have vowed to savor their singleness. They have prayed all the 31-day devotionals that are available to single Christians.

They have waited patiently for their Boaz. They have followed all the rules. They have done everything right. But it just never happened for them.

They look at other Christians who are far less committed to the Lord. They get married young and start families. They look at other single women sleeping around even though they call themselves Christians, and then eventually get married to wonderful guys. And for the life of them, they cannot understand how life could be so unfair. They lived holy. They did everything right. How could it have gone so wrong?

As they get older while remaining single, they find that they become part of a vanishing generation – older single Christians. In the church, there is a vibrant community of youths. They have no immediate interest in getting married. There are a lot of married people. They are busy with date nights and day care. But there is that shrinking in-between group – older single Christians – who seem to not fit in anywhere. They often feel lost, hopeless and displaced. As time goes by, they realize that most of the books out there are targeted toward younger singles, not the older ones. And most of all, they realize that none of the conventional advice given to single people actually work.

Yet people continue to bombard them with platitudes – *"Wait on God. He will bring to pass His perfect will in His perfect timing. God has someone really special in store for you."* But over time, these encouragements become less and less encouraging. They love the Lord and they are thankful for all that God has given them and done for them. But they feel that their life is defined by the one thing God has chosen to withhold from them. Somehow that one thing outweighs all the blessings. They even negotiate with God, *"I would give back all these blessings in an instant if you would only send me a spouse."*

We have been there

Indira and I have been there. The reason we know these emotions so well is because we have lived them. This book was not written by two people who got lucky and married their childhood sweetheart right out of high school. It was written by two people who were both over 35 when they met – yet consider their marriage to be the happiest in the world.

We both were barraged with reassurances such as *"Be patient, God has someone really special for you, just hold on."* We would politely nod and smile, but in our minds we would think, *"I don't need another promise from God. I need God to actually deliver on one of them."* One pastor even told Indira that there were no more good single men left at her age, and that God wanted to *"set her aside"* for ministry. We had long stopped believing that it would ever work out for us.

But when we finally met each other, after years of struggle and bitter disappointment, it worked out so easily. After searching for over a decade, we were married within 7 months of meeting each other. We both found that our relationship was better than anything we had ever hoped or prayed for. I remember one time during our courtship, I was in prayer and I actually burst into tears and had to repent for all the times I had doubted God. We will share much more of our story in the later chapters.

We are not writing to tickle your emotions. Yes this is a very emotional subject. We are writing to provide guidance. We are not going to add our voices to those telling you *"God has set aside someone for you."* That is not scriptural, and even if it were true (which it is not), how does knowing that help you in any way? You don't need any more encouragement. You have had enough of that. What you need is solid Biblical guidance on how to go about searching for a mate. What you need is a scripture-based action plan.

As persons who got married later in life, we have learned a lot along the way. We have learned that Christians remain single longer than they should because of myths they have believed. One such myth is the concept of *"the one."* *"The one"* is like Santa Claus. Everyone believes in it, but it is not real. It is a myth. Many Christians remain single because they are waiting for something that God never promised them, or are waiting for God when God is waiting for them. There is a time for every purpose under heaven. There is a time to wait for God, and there is a time to get up and make things happen. There are things to wait on God to do, and there are things you have to do. The Bible never promises us that God will send *"the one."* That is a man-made teaching – a myth – and this myth is keeping Christians single.

How myths keep us single

> *Now the Spirit expressly says that in latter times some will depart from the faith, giving heed to <u>deceiving spirits</u> and <u>doctrines of demons</u>, speaking lies in hypocrisy, having their own conscience seared with a hot iron, <u>forbidding to marry</u> ... (1 Timothy 4:1-3)*

This passage speaks of seducing spirits and doctrines taught by demons. One of these doctrines is forbidding others to marry. So we can conclusively state that there are demons or spirits out there who do not want good Christians to marry each other.

The next question is what is the modus operandi of these spirits? How exactly do they prevent Christians from marrying? Do they providentially prevent Christians from meeting and falling in love with other eligible

Christians? Do they force people into wrong relationships? Do they put a curse on us such that we are destined to never get married? Do they cause us to develop attitudes that make it hard to get married? And how do we deal with these spirits? Do we have to cast them out, bind them, loose them, renounce them?

1 Timothy 4 answers all of these questions. These spirits are called deceiving or seducing spirits. Their modus operandi is deception. It speaks of doctrines taught by demons. Their weapon is deceiving doctrines. Their weapon is myths that they cause Christians to believe – and that is how they keep Christians single. So the solution is not binding them or casting them out, but rather exposing the myths and knowing the truth of scripture.

That is precisely what this book is about – identifying common myths that keep Christians single longer than they need to be or cause them to make wrong choices, and replacing these myths with the truth of scripture.

If you are an older single Christian, chances are that you have given heed to a lot of these teachings. If you are a younger single Christian, be careful that you don't allow these popular teachings to make you an older single Christian.

"But I love my myths"

Another thing that I noticed is that there are many single people who defend these myths with their life. Even though these myths are keeping them single, they don't want to let go of them. This is like some kind of weird spiritual Stockholm syndrome. Not too long ago, I got a hate mail from someone who disagreed with my teaching on this subject. He went on a 923 word rant telling me how wrong I was. And this is a guy.

After reading his mail, I thought to myself, *"I think I know exactly why you are still single."* But I kept that to myself. I simply told him, *"In 900 words, you have championed the cause of the conventional wisdom commonly being taught to single Christians, but you have not made a single reference to scripture. That tells me all I need to know."*

That's what I call being wrong and strong and taking long to do it.

What you will get in this book

What you need is solid scriptural guidance. In *I Kissed Waiting Goodbye*, we teach the truth of scripture. Forget all the teachings you have heard that you can't find in the Bible. Forget the conventional wisdom. The Word of God is a light unto our path. If we must journey from singleness to married life, surely it must be the Word of God that illuminates that path. What does the BIBLE teach about this journey?

In this book, we expose and debunk the common myths single Christians have been taught – myths that are keeping them single longer than they need to be or causing them to make bad marriage choices. Then we show you what the Bible actually teaches, and how Biblical principles can help you improve your chances of finding a good husband or wife. Here are some of these myths:

- **God created someone just for me – God's perfect will**
- **God will bring this person into my life in His perfect timing**
- **I need to wait for God to bring us together**
- **The way to find a spouse is to occupy myself with God's work**
- **I need to stop dating and start waiting**
- **Finding a mate is complicated and is going to be a struggle**
- **I need to find someone who is** *"compatible"* **with me**

Chances are that you are looking for someone who is *"compatible"* with you, thinking that if you marry the *"right person"*, then you will have a happy marriage. The sad fact is that most marriages end in divorce – even marriages between Christians. And among those that don't end in divorce, not all of them are happy marriages. Even Christians who thought they married the *"right person"* have experienced abuse and adultery in their marriage.

Contrary to popular opinion, the Bible NEVER teaches that if you marry the *"right person"* or someone who is *"compatible with you"*, that you will have a happy marriage. That is a myth. The Bible NEVER presents compatibility as the key to marital bliss. Instead the Bible teaches that if ANY two genuine Christians marry, they both live godly lives, and they both exercise Biblical principles, then their marriage will be happy. The focus is never on passively waiting for the right person, but proactively working on yourself and knowing what (as opposed to whom) to look for.

In this book, we will teach you how to work on yourself. We will teach you what qualities you should look for in a potential mate. We will show you how to identify red flags that signal trouble ahead. We will also teach you some proactive things you can do to help you find a good husband or wife.

On the other extreme, perhaps you are one of those who are trying too hard to make things happen. We will also talk about the pitfalls of *"missionary dating."*

I Kissed Waiting Goodbye will answer many of the questions frequently asked by single Christians. Does God choose whom you marry? What exactly is God's perfect will? Do you need to wait for God? Do you need to hear from God? What are some things you can do to help you find a mate? How can you help that person find you? What if parents object? What about people who were previously married, but now divorced? Do the rules change for them? Is finding a husband or wife really as complicated as we make it out to be? We will address all of these things in this book.

This book is structured just like one of Paul's epistles. Because there are so many unscriptural teachings being fed to single Christians, we need to lay a proper Biblical foundation to show you what the Bible teaches about finding a marriage partner, how people in the Bible found their marriage partners, and how totally different it is from what you have probably been taught. Then later on, we will get into some more practical advice that would help you in your search.

~~~~~~

The Bible never teaches that if you marry the "right person" or someone who is "compatible with you", that you will have a happy marriage. That is a myth.

~~~~~~

Perhaps you are an older single Christian like we were. Perhaps you are a younger single Christian. Maybe, you were previously married but now divorced. We have no interest in judging anyone. However you came to be single, the principles remain exactly the same. *I Kissed Waiting Goodbye* will take you through the scriptures and teach you Biblical principles that you could use in your search for a husband or wife. If you are a parent, pastor or youth leader, this book will be a great gift or study tool for single Christians. Maybe you are already married and you think you married the wrong person. We will show you that if you understand the principles outlined in scripture, you can still have a very happy marriage.

We pray that God will use the principles in this book to lead you to a good husband or wife, and God will bless you with a wonderful marriage that is better than anything you could have ever imagined.

MYTH #1

WAITING FOR "THE ONE" THAT GOD CREATED JUST FOR YOU

In this chapter

We address the popular belief that there is someone out there that God created just for you before the foundation of the world. We will learn that the Bible actually teaches no such thing, and that God has in fact given us choices when it comes to whom we marry.

Chapter outline

- Looking for *"the one"*
- Just take a wife
- Is *"soul mates"* really a thing?
- *"The one"* makes no logical sense
- There is no perfect person
- What about Genesis 24?
- Other objections
- God has given us choices

Looking for *"the one"*

Kevin decided that he would not look for a wife, he would wait for God. He refused to even go on dates. His friends tried to match him up with single girls, but Kevin would have no part of it. There was one time he thought he had found *"the one."* He was in a relationship with someone he really loved, and she loved him too. But God *"spoke"* to him and told him, *"I created her for someone else."* He promptly obeyed and ended the relationship. Today Kevin is much older, and is still unmarried. He blames God and Christians for everything that has gone wrong in his life. Kevin believed the myth that God has a perfect match for each of us. Kevin erroneously believed in *"the one"* and blames God for the consequences of believing this myth.

This is a very popular belief being perpetrated by some very popular preachers, teachers, authors, and even TV shows. But it is not scriptural. There are popular books that reinforce this myth. These books teach women about *"the man God has for you"* and about *"waiting for your Boaz."* They teach you that God has someone that He made just for you, but you won't find him unless you do two things. You must work on yourself to make sure that you are someone that he will *"receive."* Secondly, you must know what traits to look for so that you will recognize him when you see him and not fall for the devil's substitutes.

Now absolutely you must work on yourself. Absolutely you must learn how to identify godly traits in a potential mate. Everyone knows that. In fact, we will talk much more about that later in this book. But the mistake most Christians are making is that they are looking for a specific person rather than a type of person. That's a very subtle distinction that makes the difference between a fruitful search and a futile endeavor.

In this chapter, we will examine whether God really has a specific someone that He created just for you before the foundation of the world. Or whether God wants you to exercise wisdom and make your own choices.

Just take a wife

It is a very common belief among single Christians – that before the foundation of the world when God was creating people, He matched up everyone and determined in advance who should be married to whom. Therefore there is a perfect match for you somewhere out there. Popular Christian wedding songs such as *"I wonder what God was thinking when He created you"* contribute to this belief. Many Christian romance novels are based on this idea. The question is how to find this person that God supposedly created just for you.

But I believe the more important question to ask is, does this person even exist? I seriously challenge the belief that God has created a perfect match for each one of us. That belief is not scriptural, and that belief may be keeping you single. If you are looking for one very specific person, then you may end up closing your eyes to many other potentially good mates.

There is no scripture that teaches that God foreordained or appointed people to be married to each other. The Apostle Paul said that if a woman's husband dies, *"she is free to marry anyone she wishes, but he must belong to the Lord"* (1 Corinthians 7:39, NIV). If Paul believed that God has a specific person for us to marry, he would never have said *"anyone she wishes."*

Also, you will not find any person in the Bible who embarked on a pursuit to find *"the one."* There are many cases of single people finding a husband or wife in the Bible, yet no single man or woman of God ever prayed and asked God to bring to them *"the one that He appointed for them."* Instead the Bible writers used terminology like this:

Then Abram and Nahor took wives … (Genesis 11:29)

Abraham again took a wife, and her name was Keturah … (Genesis 25:1)

Then Judah took a wife for Er his firstborn, and her name was Tamar … (Genesis 38:6)

And a man of the house of Levi went and took as wife a daughter of Levi … (Exodus 2:1)

Aaron took to himself Elisheba … as wife … (Exodus 6:23)

And Othniel the son of Kenaz … he gave him his daughter Achsah as wife … (Judges 1:13)

David … sent and proposed to Abigail, to take her as his wife … (1 Samuel 25:39)

The Biblical precedent is one where men went and took their wives. None of them agonized whether this was *"the one"* God had created for them. They just took a wife. It seemed like such a simple decision. It was nowhere near the torturous decision making process that single Christians go through today.

Now I understand that times have changed. In the Bible days, women were more or less property and did not have much say in the matter. I am certainly not advocating that we return to that culture. The point I am making is that the decision whom to marry was never intended to be a travailing decision after traversing the long and winding road. It was a simple decision. No one in the Bible thought they were marrying God's perfect match for them. They just got married. We don't need to go back to Bible days, but we do need to understand Biblical principles.

Is "soul mates" really a thing?

We all love the idea of soul mates. We all want to feel like we married someone that God created just for us. But the idea of soul mates is not really a scriptural concept. The concept of a soul mate traces back to the belief that God has someone that He created just for you. The concept of a soul mate is a matter of perception.

I consider my wife Indira and me to be soul mates. It FEELS that way. If ever there was a female version of me, it would be Indira. But I also understand that this is a matter of perception. It is not a theological fact. It is one thing to feel this way after you're married, but if you make this a requirement before you marry someone, you will probably be single for a very long time.

At our wedding, we played Savage Garden's song *"I knew I loved you before I met you, I think I dreamed you into life."* It truly felt that way. Indira teasingly said that my baby pictures weren't really me, because it felt to her as though God created me in the year 2009 just for her. Again, it is one thing to feel this way, as long as you understand that this is just a feeling and not reality. It is only a perception. Songs like *"I wonder what God was thinking when He created you"* are really nice songs. But don't build your life on the words of a song. Build your belief system only on what the Word of God says.

Take these songs with a pinch of salt. They are nice and melodious and emotional, but they are not always based on sound Biblical theology. Don't make your life into a song, otherwise you'll end up right here waiting while you wish upon a star, wishing and hoping, wondering what God was thinking, and hoping that love can see you through. Stop it! Learn what the Bible teaches, and set your expectations on what God promised, not what you read in some book or heard in some song.

"The one" makes no logical sense

The belief that God has one perfect match that He created just for you before the foundation of the world is not only unscriptural, it is also not logical. Let us just pretend for a minute that when God was hatching His plan for mankind, He matched up every pair of humans such that everyone has a perfect match that He created just for them. Just pretend.

Immediately we have a problem, because there are more women than men in the world. There are more women than men in Christianity. There are likely more women than men in the church you attend. Immediately that poses a huge problem. Many people are not going to get matched according to this system.

A second problem is this. Suppose God created Jane to be married to John, Jane gets saved, but John never gets saved. Then what? Is Jane supposed to marry an unsaved person? That is something God expressly commands us not to do. What if John dies before they ever meet, what then? Should Jane remain single all her life? Or marry outside of God's *"perfect will"*? What if John marries someone else, what then? God's plan is quickly going to fall apart. What if Jane and John do get married, but then one of them dies, then what? Is Jane allowed to remarry? According to the Bible, the answer is an emphatic yes. But according to the myth that John and Jane were created for each other, then any remarriage would place Jane outside of God's perfect will.

That's how you know a belief is unscriptural – when you take it to the logical limit and you see how it falls apart under deeper scrutiny. That's why we have courts of law. Witnesses could say anything they want, but how well does their testimony hold up under cross examination?

The mistake most Christians are making is that they are looking for a specific person rather than a type of person

If God matched up people before the foundation of the world, then that plan has to be the worst plan ever. It is not sustainable. We have seen in a simple example involving just two persons how fragile this plan is. Extend it now to 7 billion people. All it takes is one person to marry outside of God's will, then that triggers a domino effect and the whole thing crumbles to the ground. In the end nobody is going to marry God's perfect match for them. It cannot work. It is a terrible plan, and our God is a wise God.

God did not create people for each other. If you are married to someone who seems to have been created just for you, that's great. I am also married to someone like that. But that is a perception, not a reality. Mind you, it is a very good perception. I wish every married person could share that feeling. But that is all it is – a feeling.

Have you ever asked someone how their food tastes? There is nothing they could possibly tell you that would communicate taste. It is impossible.

Taste is subjective. How food tastes to one person is different from how it tastes to someone else. The same thing is true with soul mates. You may feel like soul mates after you get married. It may feel as though God created you just for each other. But that feeling is like a taste. You cannot then make that a rule for everyone else. You cannot tell them that if they don't have the same feelings, then they are out of God's will.

Unfortunately, this is precisely what popular teachers are doing. They found their husband or wife a certain way, and they are now teaching that everyone else must find their husband or wife the same way.

I feel that Indira and I are soul mates. It seems as though I dreamed her into life, and that when God created her, He was thinking about me. But that is just a feeling. I cannot teach that to single people who are looking for a mate. They will end up getting the wrong impression, and may end up setting such unrealistic expectations, that they may never get married. I must teach what the Bible teaches – God did not create any perfect match. He gives us choices, and wisdom and guidance to make the best decision.

There is no perfect person

Many Christians remain single because they have unrealistic expectations. Some expect too much from a marriage partner. Others expect too much from the marriage relationship, and end up disappointed when they realize that marriage is not solving all of their problems. Of course, there is nothing wrong with setting high standards. You absolutely should set high standards. You should never settle. You should never marry someone you don't love or someone who is not what you are looking for simply because you are afraid to end up alone. You will just end up miserable for the rest of your life, or divorced.

However, you should not set unreasonably high standards that no human being can meet. Your expectations should be high, but not unrealistic. For example, if you are generally an unhappy person, no husband or wife is going to swoop into your life and turn your sorrow into joy. No one is going to transform your darkness into light with a magic kiss. This is not Sleeping Beauty. This is real life. In real life, two people get married and in addition to the joy they bring to each other, they also bring a lot of baggage.

One of the reasons Christians set unrealistically high expectations is because they believe that God has a perfect match that He will bring into their lives in His perfect timing. If you believe that God has someone that He predestined to be your husband, then you would naturally expect this person to be a tall, dark prince. It will be awfully difficult for you to believe that of all the people on this planet that God ordained for you, it would be a short stocky bald broke guy who is OK looking at best. How could God's will for you be George Costanza? As a result, you will keep turning down anyone who is not called William or Harry.

Let me bring you back down to earth. Unless your name is Kate Middleton or Meghan Markle, you are probably not going to marry a prince – unless you want to be a 3rd wife in somebody's harem. You are most likely going to marry a very ordinary person with flaws and shortcomings ... just like yourself. And you know what? I prefer someone with flaws any day over someone who is perfect.

The belief that God has a perfect mate out there for us is the very reason many Christians are single. It is because that belief is a myth. It creates all sorts of unreasonable expectations that are so far removed from reality, that you will never find happiness with any human being. You need to rid your mind of this misguided belief that there is a perfect mate for you that God ordained before the foundation of the world. That is a myth that may be keeping you single. Once you dispel that myth, you will be transformed from the land of fairy tales back to real life.

There are even married people who feel that they married the wrong person, or that someone else was indeed God's perfect match for them. Because of this belief, they never really get to enjoy their marriage. They are forever living in some parallel universe in their mind. Even though they are married, this myth is keeping them as if they were single. No wonder the Bible calls it doctrines taught by demons. It is truly incorrect beliefs that are responsible for a lot of problems we face in life.

I know of many married people who are angry with God because the husband that *"God gave them"* is not as good as the husband He gave somebody else. Their big assumption is that God gave them that husband, when in fact it was their choice.

What about Genesis 24?

Earlier I noted that there is no man or woman of God in the Bible who ever prayed for the *"one that God appointed for them."* Depending on how well you know the Bible, you might have thought about Genesis 24:14, where Abraham sent a servant to find a wife for Isaac, and the servant prayed these words:

> *... let her be <u>the one You have appointed</u> for Your servant Isaac ... (Genesis 24:14)*

Whenever someone – including me – comes to you with something that sounds different from what you have heard before, I strongly recommend that you search the scriptures to see if what they are saying is true. This scripture seems to suggest that there was a wife that God had appointed for Isaac.

Now let us look more closely at Genesis 24. Abraham was getting old and Isaac was still single. So being the typical meddlesome parent, Abraham decided to take matters into his own hands and find a wife for Isaac. He got his servant and sent him on a mission to his home town to find a wife for Isaac. Notice the instruction that Abraham gave to the servant.

> *I will make you swear by the Lord, the God of heaven and the God of the earth, that you will not take a wife for my son from the daughters of the Canaanites, among whom I dwell; but you shall go to my country and to my family, and <u>take a wife for my son Isaac</u>. … The Lord God of heaven … <u>He will send His angel before you</u>, and <u>you shall take a wife for my son from there</u>. … (Genesis 24:3,4,7)*

In Abraham's instruction to the servant, there was no mention of *"the one God appointed for Isaac."* He simply told the servant to *"take a wife for my son Isaac"* and that God would go before him to guide him. Abraham who knew God and was a friend of God, simply believed that God would go before him and guide him as the servant chose a wife for Isaac.

The servant then decided that he wanted to pray for himself. In his prayer, he addressed God as the *"Lord God of my master Abraham"*, and he prayed for God to send the one that God appointed. This was the servant's prayer.

> *"<u>O Lord God of my master Abraham</u>, please give me success this day, and show kindness to my master Abraham. Behold, here I stand by the well of water, and the daughters of the men of the city are coming out to draw water. Now let it be that the young woman to whom I say, 'Please let down your pitcher that I may drink,' and she says, 'Drink, and I will also give your camels a drink' – let her be <u>the one You have appointed for Your servant Isaac</u>. And by this I will know that You have shown kindness to my master." … (Genesis 24:12-14)*

The first thing to note about the servant is that he did not know God intimately. If he did, he would have addressed God as *"My Lord God"* not *"Lord God of my master."* Secondly, he did not know how God operated. So he essentially cast lots to determine who Isaac's wife would be.

Do you remember in Acts 1, after Judas died, the apostles had to select someone to replace him? They did not as yet have the Holy Spirit, so they had no clue what to do. They decided to cast lots to make their decision – essentially they flipped a coin. But after they received the Holy Spirit, God would speak to them openly. They never had to cast lots after that. Casting lots is not the best way to hear from God, but God may honor it if His plan of redemption depends on it.

Abraham's servant gave God a semi-random test and whoever passed that test, he assumed that would be *"the one."* That was a huge assumption, but because God's plan of redemption was invested in this, God honored his prayer. But that is not an indication of how we should pray. I certainly do not advise you to pray to God and say, *"Lord, the first woman who smiles with me today, please let her be my future wife."* That's just being weird – serial killer weird.☺

Jean was dating a guy called Benny who was not really saved, and she wanted to know whether he was *"the one"* for her. Benny had said the sinner's prayer, but he showed no sign of commitment or growth. But in Jean's mind, saying the sinner's pray was enough. One night he accompanied her to church, and Jean asked God for a sign. *"Lord, if he lifts his hands in church tonight, I will take that as a sign that he is the one."* During the worship service, the song leader said, *"Everybody lift your hands to God and give Him praise."*

Don't be like Jean. Don't pray to God like that. Abraham's servant clearly did not know God and how God operated. He simply prayed for God to move according to his level of thinking. With all due respect to him, he was wrong. The guy who did not know God prayed for *"the one that God had appointed"*, while the guy who was a friend of God simply commanded him to *"take a wife."* In whose prayer do you have more confidence? Would you rather have the faith of the man who did not know God or the man who was a friend of God?

This scripture does not teach that God has an appointed husband or wife for anyone. It only notes that Abraham's servant believed this. This does not make him correct.

What Genesis 24 does teach however, is that God guides us and gives us wisdom to choose. Abraham did believe that God would go before him, but stopped short of believing that God had an appointed wife for Isaac. Put the pieces together. <u>Abraham sent his servant to *"take a wife"* under God's guidance. That is how we ought to be looking for a husband or wife.</u> Don't waste your time looking for *"the one whom God appointed for you."* That one does not exist. Instead, trust God to guide you and give you wisdom as you look for a husband or wife.

We will talk more about Isaac and Rebekah later on since there are many important principles in that passage of scripture that will help you in your search.

Other objections

"Well what about Jeremiah 29:11?" you ask in a whiny nasal voice.☺

> *For I know the thoughts that I think toward you, saith the Lord, thoughts of peace, and not of evil, to give you an expected end … (Jeremiah 29:11, KJV)*

This is a wonderful verse of scripture. But does this mean that only good things will happen to us and God will not let anything bad come our way? Tell that to Stephen who got stoned to death because of Jesus. The entire book of Jeremiah is a sad book. The author is called the weeping prophet. Why do we take the one happy verse in the entire book and act as though Jeremiah only has one verse?

I hate to be a kill-joy, but that verse is not really talking about our personal lives. It is talking about the nation of Israel. God is promising that in a future time, He will restore Israel and set up His eternal kingdom. Jeremiah 29:11 is called a millennial prophecy. It is a promise to Israel that they will have a good ending. This is a very common motif in Bible prophecy.

But this verse speaks of Israel's END, not their journey. It turns out that Israel's journey has been very rocky. They were soon thereafter tossed into captivity in Babylon, then they had to endure an oppressive Roman regime, and later on there was the little issue of the holocaust. But God will eventually restore them and give them an expected end. The expected end does not mean that God will reward you with a husband or wife after you endure your trial of singleness. It's not talking about our personal lives.

If you are in Christ, you will have an *"expected end"* when you are resurrected. That expected end is not your wedding day. But the in-between (your life on earth) – this verse says nothing about that. You have to exercise the principles of scripture and make your life on earth what you want it to be. You need to be proactive and work for what you want.

"Well doesn't the Bible say seek not a wife?" you ask in a whiny nasal voice.☺ Yes the Bible does say,

> *Are you bound to a wife? Do not seek to be loosed. Are you loosed from a wife? Do not seek a wife … (1 Corinthians 7:27)*

If you read the entire chapter for context, you will see that Paul is NOT saying that we should *"seek not a wife"* because God will bring a wife to us. That would be missing the point big time. Paul is saying, *"Don't seek a wife AT ALL because of the present distress and because the time is short."* Paul is telling the Corinthians that because of their present distress (whatever that was), they should not seek to make major changes in their lives – if you're married stay married, if you're single stay single. But that was not a general rule for every Christian. Paul made that rule for himself, and he advised the Corinthians to do the same IF THEY COULD. If not, then marry.

"Well doesn't the Bible say to wait on the Lord?" you ask in a whiny nasal voice.☺ Yes the Bible does say to wait on the Lord, but again that does not mean that we do nothing while we wait. We have to do what we can do, and trust and wait on God to do what He has to do. Waiting on God is not passive.

"But doesn't God know the future?" you ask in a whiny nasal voice.☺ Yes God does know the future. But God knowing the future and God predetermining the future are two entirely different things.

Suppose God told you that at age 42 you will be a millionaire, what will you do with that knowledge? More than likely, you will relax and become complacent – coast until you are 42. However, if you did not know the future, you would be working hard, investing wisely and making good contacts. And these are the actions that God requires of you so that He can prosper you. So then, wouldn't it be best if God kept the future hidden from us?

The point I am making is that knowing your future is not likely to do you any good. God wants us to live by faith, not by revelation. Faith is the evidence of things hoped for (Hebrews 11:1) and hope that is seen is not hope (Romans 8:24). In other words, God does not want us to live revelation-to-revelation, but rather by faith in what He has chosen to reveal for a future we cannot see.

God knows whom, if and when you will marry. But unless you know what God knows, then what God knows does not profit you in anyway. We cannot build our lives on what God knows, but rather what He has revealed. God is omniscient – He knows everything. 1 Corinthians 13:9 clearly teaches that we only know in part. In other words, God is not going to reveal everything to you. Do what the Bible teaches even if you don't know the future, and trust Him to do what He promised. You don't need a revelation from God to get married. More on this in Myth #3.

God has given us choices

The Biblical reality is that there is no one person that God created and appointed just for you. That is not how God works. God gave us choices. There are many possible people you could be married to. If you are looking for one specific person, you have made the process a lot more difficult than it is supposed to be. No one in the Bible went looking for one specific individual, waiting for God's perfect match. They just took a wife.

What Christians should be looking for is not *"the one"*, but rather *"the type."* You should not be looking for one specific person that you perceive to be God's perfect match created just for you. That person is fictitious. That's like waiting for James Bond – he is not real. There are many people who could be a good husband or wife for you. You should be looking for one of them, rather than *"the one."*

Now I need to clarify that I am NOT saying that you could be married to more than one person at the same time. I am absolutely NOT saying that. I preached this message once and people came away with the idea that I was advocating polygamy. I am NOT advocating polygamy.

The common myth Christians believe is that there is only one specific person God created for you and you need to find that specific person, otherwise you would be outside of God's perfect will. I am saying that there are many people that are eligible mates for you, and you need to marry ONE of them. There is no *"one right person."* Instead there are many people who would be good mates for you, just marry any one of them. There are also many people who would not be good mates for you, avoid them like the plague.

"Well what about God's perfect will?" you ask in a whiny nasal voice.☺ That's what the next chapter is about.

MYTH #2

WAITING FOR "GOD'S PERFECT WILL IN GOD'S PERFECT TIMING"

In this chapter

We will learn about God's will. What exactly is the will of God? What is God's perfect will? Is it a detailed blueprint for our lives? We will learn that God's will is not as rigid as we think. God's will is general and broad, and has a lot of flexibility built into it.

Chapter outline

- Who cares about blueprints?
- God does not care about blueprints
- What exactly is God's will?
- What is God's perfect will?
- God's will is not spooky spiritual
- Three aspects of God's will
- God does have a plan for your life
- God's will is flexible
- God's will is post-determined not pre-determined
- What was God's will for the Apostle Paul?
- What is God's will for single Christians today?
- Don't take my word for it

Who cares about blueprints?

Some friends of ours recently decided to build an extension to their house. They contacted a number of contractors, described to them what they wanted and asked for a cost estimate. There were two of them that stood out for different reasons. One was from a professional architect who looked at the space, inspected the compound, and later sent a quote via email that looked something like this:

Site visit	$1,000
Architectural plans / blueprints	$10,000
Painting	$40,000
Drain repair	$17,000
Equipment rentals	$17,000
Construction Cost	to be determined after site visit
TOTAL	**$85,000 + construction cost**

When our friends saw the email, they started looking around their house for hidden cameras. They were certain they were on a TV prank show. Was this guy joking or was he really charging $10,000 for blueprints? They didn't care about blueprints and architectural drawings. They weren't trying to build the Empire State Building, just an additional living room in their house. Blueprints were overkill. It was a waste of money. A simple sketch was sufficient for the level of work they were interested in.

The second quote was from a freelance construction worker. His quote looked something like this:

Drainage	$5,000
Building the foundation	$25,000
Construction cost	$23,000
Painting	$25,000
TOTAL	$78,000

Which one of them do you think got the job? The guy who was charging half the price, or the guy who was charging $10,000 for blueprints? This was one of the easiest decisions they ever had to make.

The moral of this story is that sometimes in life, you don't need blueprints. A simple outline is good enough.

God does not care about blueprints

Many people live their lives as if God had a detailed blueprint for every minute of every day of their lives. They believe that every minute detail of their lives was predetermined by God before the foundation of the world. This includes what they have for breakfast on any given day, which path they take to go to work, which job they accept, and the person they marry — all foreordained by God before the foundation of the world. Every decision becomes an agonizing ordeal. *"Is it God's will for me to take the freeway or the back streets? Lord please speak to me right now."*

This is not how God works. God does not have a detailed blueprint for our personal lives. Instead God has more of a 5-point plan for the redemption of mankind.

1) God created man in His image and likeness
2) God sent Jesus to die for our sins
3) The Holy Spirit raised Jesus from the dead
4) God sent the Holy Spirit to the church on the Day of Pentecost
5) Jesus will return to set up His eternal kingdom

That's it. That is God's blueprint. I'm pretty sure God could have sketched this out with a pencil. History is defined by these crucial moments, and God does not micromanage the in-betweens.

Here is an important principle that teaches how God works. God created Adam from the dust and He created Eve from Adam's rib. But every human being who was ever born afterward, came through natural procreation. God never created anyone else the same way. After the initial creation, God left man in charge. For the most part, God allows the world to run on autopilot, stepping in occasionally to do what needs to be done. That is how God works. God is in control, but He does not micromanage every single detail of history.

The belief that God has a perfect will for every aspect of your life, is based on a misunderstanding of God's will. This misunderstanding will cause you to look for the wrong thing in the wrong way.

This myth makes us believe that our detailed daily walk is foreordained by God, and if we just keep walking each day in his perfect detailed will, and *"the one"* also walks in this detailed perfect will, then one day your paths will intersect at a divinely foreordained place and time, you will get married, and then you must now continue to walk along a divinely ordained detailed path together. Phew! This myth is as tiring as that sentence is long.

What exactly is God's will?

God's will is a very much misunderstood concept in scripture. Many people make the mistake of believing that God's will is a detailed blueprint for their lives that God ordained before the foundation of the world. Whoever follows this blueprint has achieved God's perfect will – God's best. The others are in God's permissive will. As a result, every decision they make is met with the questions *"Is this God's will? What is God's will in this situation?"* Some people take this to the ridiculous limit and won't make any decision unless they *"hear from God."* This is especially true for what they perceive to be the more important decisions in life, for example, whom they should marry.

Not surprisingly, these folk also believe that God has a specific person chosen before the foundation of the world for them to marry. Marriage then becomes the most agonizing decision of their lives. They will be sitting next to someone in class and wonder *"Is this person God's will for me?"*

Once at a church singles group meeting, the members were playing a game that allowed them to get to know each other. They were randomly paired with members of the opposite sex to ask and answer a few simple questions. In one group, I overheard the girl asking the guy, *"Isn't it strange that we got paired up? Do you think it is God's will?"* The guy wasn't really sure what to say, so he just moved on to question #1. It was painful to watch.

I know of another woman who was at the altar in her church praying with a picture of her boyfriend in her hand. Another church member saw the picture and told her *"He is not the one. He is not God's will for you."* She proceeded to end the relationship based on that *"word."* Now was that word from God? Maybe, maybe not. Maybe she dodged a bullet, or maybe she missed out on the love of a lifetime. It is impossible for me to tell. But that is based on a misconception that there is such a thing as God's perfect will for marriage.

What is God's perfect will?

Traditionally, whenever Bible teachers talk about God's will, they make a distinction between God's perfect will and God's permissive will. According to this teaching, God's perfect will is what God wants for your life – God's best. His permissive will is what He permits even though it was not His first choice. For example, they teach you that a specific person is God's perfect will for your husband or wife. However, if you marry someone else, then God permits it even though it was not His first choice for you. That would be God's permissive will because He merely permitted it.

So some Christians are in God's perfect will while others are only in God's permissive will. Some married couples are in God's perfect will because they married the person that God chose for them, while others are only in God's permissive will because they married someone of their own choosing.

This teaching is very popular but NOT completely scriptural. It often comes across as elitist. The couples who married according to God's perfect will are deemed to be in a higher spiritual standing than those who merely married according to God's permissive will. God is pleased with those who are in His perfect will, but He merely puts up with those in His permissive will.

Yes the term perfect will of God does appear in the Bible, but it does not refer to a blueprint that God ordained for each one of us. Further, the term permissive will does not appear anywhere in the Bible. I should also point out that if God's permissive will is whatever God allows, then technically everything that happens is God's permissive will, because nothing could happen if God does not permit it.

God's will is not so much about what you do, but how you do it

This teaching is based on a misinterpretation of Romans 12:2. This teaching leads to a gross misunderstanding of the will of God. And this is keeping a lot of Christians from getting married.

> *I beseech you therefore, brethren, by the mercies of God, that you present your bodies a living sacrifice, holy, acceptable to God, which is your reasonable service. And do not be conformed to this world, but be transformed by the renewing of your mind, that you may prove what is that good and acceptable and <u>perfect will of God</u> ... (Romans 12:1-2)*

Let me explain what that scripture means. Notice the word *"therefore"* at the beginning of verse 1. This means that what Paul is about to tell them is a result of what he told them in the previous chapters – specifically in this case chapters 9 – 11. In the Roman church, there was a conflict between the Jewish Christians and the Gentile Christians. The Jews were boasting *"We are God's chosen people"*, while the Gentiles were boasting, *"Yeah but God rejected you all, we are now God's people."* Paul is admonishing them not to boast. The Gentiles should not boast because they were not originally God's people. The Jews should not boast because they were God's people all these years, yet they still disobeyed Him. No one should boast because everyone has sinned and come short of the glory of God.

Paul is talking about the Jews and the Gentiles and the place they hold in God's master plan. God initially chose the Jews, but they rejected Him. So He temporarily rejected Israel and offered salvation to the Gentiles. In so doing, God hopes to provoke Israel to a holy jealousy so they would return to Him. In the end, God would use everyone's disobedience, turn it around for good, and end up saving both Jews and Gentiles.

For God has committed them all to disobedience, that He might have mercy on all ... (Romans 11:32)

When Paul thought about the wisdom and elegance of God's master plan for the salvation of mankind, he exclaimed:

Oh, the depth of the riches both of the wisdom and knowledge of God! How unsearchable are His judgments and His ways past finding out! ... (Romans 11:33)

Then he continues in chapter 12, admonishing the church not to be conformed to the world but be transformed by the renewing of their minds, proving what is that good and acceptable and perfect will of God.

Do you think after Paul went to such great lengths to talk about the Jews and the Gentiles and God's master plan for mankind, that he would turn to them and say, *"Hey guys, guess what. God has a perfect will and a permissive will. Do God's perfect will OK."* Seriously?

Paul is actually telling the church not to be like the world where people are always competing with each other and cutting each other down. Instead you need to renew your mind – change your attitude and your way of thinking. Instead of competing and pulling down each other, recognize what God's master plan is. God is bringing his sheep together, so condition your thinking accordingly. Work together, cooperate with each other, help each other out. Change your way of thinking in the light of God's master plan.

Bottom line: God's perfect will is not a blueprint that God ordained for your life before the foundation of the world. It refers to God's master plan for mankind. This plan is good, acceptable and perfect.

God's will is not spooky spiritual

The popular teaching about God's perfect and permissive will causes Christians to be passive and to not use wisdom. It also ends up dividing Christians into the super spiritual ones with whom God is well pleased, and the so-so ones whom God merely tolerates. There are the so-called spiritual ones – those who were able to hear from God and obey His perfect will. Then there are the unspiritual ones who make their own decisions, don't follow God's blueprint, and live in the flesh. They must settle for God's permissive will.

Ironically, that divisive elitist attitude is the very thing that Paul was trying to discourage in the Roman church. Instead of thinking of yourselves as better than others, start thinking in terms of how you can love and serve others. Present yourself as a living sacrifice just as Christ presented Himself as a dying sacrifice.

Elsewhere, Paul taught that true spirituality is not the ability to *"hear from God"* but remaining humble and helping your fellow believers without being unduly judgmental.

> *Brethren, if a man is overtaken in any trespass, you who are spiritual restore such a one in a spirit of gentleness, considering yourself lest you also be tempted. Bear one another's burdens, and so fulfill the law of Christ. For if anyone thinks himself to be something, when he is nothing, he deceives himself. ... (Galatians 6:1-3)*

As you read the scriptures, you won't find this division between the so-called spiritual Christians and the unspiritual ones. The only division the Bible makes is between genuine Christians and fake Christians / non-Christians. We are all imperfect people redeemed by the blood of Christ working together until Christ returns.

So if you are trying to find God's perfect match in God's perfect timing by following some blueprint that God outlined for your life before time began, you are following a major misinterpretation of Romans 12. That blueprint only exists in your mind. This, my friends, is a myth that is keeping Christians single because you end up waiting for and expecting things that God never promised.

Three aspects of God's will

God's plan for mankind is very basic and very general. Man sinned and God wants to save man from his sins. That's about the gist of it. As I study the scriptures, I find three aspects of God's will or God's plan for mankind:
1) What God does on His own
2) What God providentially works out
3) What God commands us to do

What God does on His own
There are a handful of events that God ordained before the foundation of the world.
1) Jesus Christ was slain before the foundation of the world (1 Peter 1:20; Revelation 13:8)
2) We were chosen in Him before the foundation of the world (Ephesians 1:4) – our calling and election that is.
3) God prepared His kingdom for us before the foundation of the world (Matthew 25:34)

These are critical incidents in God's plan of redemption. These are things that must happen in order for God to execute His master plan. So how does God ensure that they come to pass? He does them Himself. He does not command us to make any of them happen. He does not depend on our cooperation to make any of them come to pass. God makes them happen on His own.

Notice that our husbands or wives are not on this list, because the Bible does not teach that God matches up people before the foundation of the world. That is a non-critical aspect of God's plan where God is flexible.

God's providence
The second aspect of God's will is called providence. This refers to God quietly working things out in the background without directly intervening.

When Paul was on the road to Damascus, God directly intervened and stopped him in his tracks. Then later on, God called for Paul and Barnabas to be released for the work He called them to do. That was God making something happen. This was not providence, but rather a direct intervention of God.

But once Paul answered the call to be an apostle, how did he determine where he should travel to on any given day? He simply went wherever there was opportunity. On one occasion, God directed him to Macedonia via a dream (Acts 16:9). On another occasion, He wanted to go to Thessalonica, but Satan hindered him (1 Thessalonians 2:8). He just went somewhere else. Paul also prayed for God to make a way according to His will for him to visit the church in Rome (Romans 1:10).

This illustrates the difference between God's providence and God's direct intervention. God gives us general guidelines – go and preach the gospel. Where exactly? Anywhere you get an opportunity. If God needs to give you specific directions, He will. But preaching the gospel does not require specific directions. God will work silently in the background causing you to go where He wants you to. God may close one door and open another door.

I am sure you have heard the story of the man who was drowning, but he maintained strong faith that God would save him. One guy came with a boat, but he refused. *"I am waiting for God!"* A helicopter flew by and dropped the ladder. *"No, God will save me."* Of course he drowned. Then he went to heaven (because we are saved by grace and not by being smart), and he asked God, *"Why didn't you save me?"* God answered, *"I sent you a boat and a helicopter. What else did you want me to do?"*

This is an example of God's providence. He sent a boat and a helicopter, but He did come down directly to save the man from drowning. God's providence is a much underrated aspect of God's will. Yet MOST of God's operations happens through providence than through any other means. Chances are that you will live most of your life through God's providence. Maybe God will directly intervene once or twice in your lifetime, maybe never at all. But God's hand is always at work in the background, causing things to work together for your good, causing His will to happen.

I am certain you have heard that story before. I guess you never thought it was talking about you, huh? Many of you are single because you are waiting for specifics rather than following the general principles that God has outlined in His word.

What God commands us to do

The third aspect of God's will is what God commands us to do.
1) God wants all to be saved and none to be lost (1 Timothy 2:4; 2 Peter 3:9)
2) God's will is that we believe in Christ (John 6:29,40)
3) God's will is that we work for Him in His kingdom (Matthew 21:31)
4) God's will is that we live holy transformed lives on this earth (1 Thessalonians 4:3)

5) God's will is that we do good and be an example to others (1 Peter 2:15)
6) God's will is that we endure suffering for the sake of His gospel (1 Peter 3:17)

Notice how broad it is. For example in the parable in Matthew 21:31, the master simply told his sons *"come and work."* That's it. He did not give them a specific agenda or job description. His will was simply that they worked for him.

Does God want you to be an engineer, a lawyer, or a doctor? The answer is none of the above, not applicable. God's will is that you work. This plan is not very specific. It is deliberately general. God has a lot of leeway built into His plan. What you do for a living is not high on God's list of priorities. God just wants you to work. Whatever you do, do it as unto the Lord, serving God from your heart. This is God's will concerning your job.

And <u>whatever you do</u>, do it heartily, as to the Lord and not to men ... (Colossians 3:23)

If God had a specific job for you that was His perfect will, Paul would have never used the words *"whatever you do."* In other words, <u>God's will is not so much about WHAT you do for a living, but HOW you do it</u>. Did you get that?

Whom does God want me to marry? The only thing God commands of us is that we marry a fellow Christian of the opposite gender. Believe it or not, that is the only command God gave us concerning whom to marry. But once you get married, God's will is that wives submit to their husbands and husbands love their wives. Do you get how God's will works?

<u>God does have a plan for your life</u>

Now let's pause for a moment and add some perspective to all of this. God does have a plan for our lives. However that plan is not rigidly engraved in stone. That plan does not have to make us anxious about missing God's perfect will. Every decision does not have to be a burdensome ordeal.

God determines where and when we were born (Acts 17:26). God gives us gifts and callings. He works in us both to will and to do His good pleasure (Philippians 2:13). In other words, God puts thoughts, desires and proclivities in us that cause us to do what He wants us to do. God providentially opens and closes doors (Revelation 3:8).

All of these things together with God's instructions in the Bible are sufficient to lead us into God's will. As long as we are led by the Spirit of God, we will automatically be in God's will. God's will does not have to be a source of worry, frustration and anxiety. Just follow the leading of the Holy Spirit in your life, do what the Word of God says, and you will be OK concerning God's will.

God does care about us. He cares about our burdens and sorrows. He instructed us to cast our cares on Him. But at the same time, not everything has equal importance in God's plan. Whether or not I get married may be a huge deal to me, it is not a huge deal to God. Again, whom I marry may be a very big deal to me, it is a not-so-big deal to God. It is not a small deal, more like a medium sized deal to God. Whether or not I marry and whomever I marry do not affect God's master plan for the world. They do not. Let's not be presumptuous by thinking more of ourselves than we ought to. We need to put things in their proper perspective otherwise we will end up making this decision harder than it needs to be – which you probably already have done.

God's will is flexible

The belief that every aspect of history is predestined and micromanaged by God is what I refer to as hyper-Calvinism or if you wish, Calvinism-on-caffeine. This is what the reformer John Calvin would teach if he had just a little too much coffee to drink.

Calvin taught that God predestines people to heaven or to hell. God says *"eenie meenie minie mo"* and He picks and chooses before the foundation of the world who would go to heaven and who would go to hell. Those He predestined to heaven, He drags them by their ears to repentance and saves them. The rest, He merely leaves them to their own devices, and they never get saved. You could tell from the tone of my writing that I do not agree with the theology of John Calvin.

Nevertheless, it is one thing to believe that God predestines individuals to either be saved or not be saved. This is a very valid belief, although, it is debatable. Many prominent theologians do not agree with John Calvin. I am not going to address that issue in this book, but here is what I would like to point out. Predestination deals with salvation and election. The doctrine of election is about who gets called to salvation and who does not get called. You cannot take predestination outside of this context. You cannot say that God predestines every decision we make. That is Calvinism-on-caffeine – taking predestination outside the context of salvation and applying it to every aspect of our lives. It is borderline fatalism. Not even John Calvin believed that – unless of course, he had too much coffee.

The fact is that there are some aspects of God's plan that are subject to change, and some that are not. History is punctuated by major events and minor events. Major events would include God sending Christ into the world, Jesus dying for our sins, and Christ returning to set up His eternal kingdom. Those are the major events. These aspects of God's will do not change. God guarantees they will come to pass because He will bring them to pass Himself.

Then there are minor details of history that do not really impinge on God's master plan. For example, if I got saved at age 50 rather than age 19, would that delay Christ's second coming? The answer is no. The age I got saved is a minor detail in history that is subject to variability – God's plan will be accomplished either way.

So regarding the major aspects of God's plan, God does not change His mind. They are fixed. Regarding the minor aspects, God has flexibility and He gives us leeway. Things like whom we marry, when we marry, what job we do, which path we take to get to work – these are all minor details which do not affect God's master plan. God is flexible regarding whom you marry providing that you marry a fellow Christian.

God's will is post-determined not pre-determined

Based on what the Bible teaches, God's will concerning marriage is post-determined rather than pre-determined. Pre-determined means that God decides in advance that something will happen – before the foundation of the world. Whom we marry is not one of those things. God does not decide in advance who will marry whom, and when this will happen. He gives us a tremendous amount of leeway in choosing whom and when we marry. Then once we marry, God puts His stamp of approval on it and says *"This is now my will, and what I join together let no one separate."* It becomes His will after the fact.

What if you marry the wrong person, then what? Well if you believe that God has a perfect husband or wife that He created just for you, then if you marry the wrong person, that puts you in a bit of a problem. Should you just continue in the *"wrong marriage"*? Should you divorce the *"wrong husband or wife"* and marry the right one?

None of these questions matter if you truly understand God's will. God does not have a perfect person for you, nor does He have a right person for you. God gives you choices. If you marry someone, then that becomes

God's will. Even if you make a bad decision, it still becomes God's will after the fact. It is post-determined. There is no question of divorcing that person to marry someone else ... unless there is infidelity.

Even if you marry an unsaved person, these principles do not change. The Bible makes it abundantly clear that if you are married to an unsaved person who is willing to abide with you, you are not to divorce that person.

> *If any brother has a wife who does not believe, and she is willing to live with him, let him not divorce her. And a woman who has a husband who does not believe, if he is willing to live with her, let her not divorce him ... 1 (Corinthians 7:12-13)*

God desires that we marry fellow Christians. He admonishes us to marry fellow Christians. But IF we marry an unsaved person, God does not give us the option to divorce them on the basis that they are unsaved. This would be contrary to the Word of God (will of God). Although we would have gone against God's wishes and God's commands, the marriage still becomes God's will.

Are you seeing the difference between God's will and God's desires? Even though God did not want us to marry the unsaved person in the first place, if He wanted us to divorce that person and remarry a Christian, then He would have never inspired Paul to write 1 Corinthians 7:13. This is an example where God's will concerning a minor event changes according to the situation. But His master plan remains unaffected and on-course.

What was God's will for the Apostle Paul?

The Apostle Paul was single. Was it God's will for Paul to remain single? Or was it God's will for Paul to get married, and if so, to whom? Can we answer these questions from the Bible? Believe it or not, we actually can.

Paul said that he and Barnabas could have taken wives if they wanted to. But Paul chose to remain single.

> *Do we have no right to take along a believing wife, as do also the other apostles? ... Nevertheless we have not used this right, but endure all things lest we hinder the gospel of Christ ... (1 Corinthians 9:5,12)*

Let's look at the possibilities.

1. Was it God's will for Paul to remain single?

If so, then Paul was out of place to say he could have married if he wanted to. If God ordained Paul to be single, then Paul had no choice but to remain single. But Paul was writing under the inspiration of the Holy Spirit. So we can conclude that Paul was not out of place. Therefore, it was not God's will for Paul to remain single.

2. So then, was it God's will for Paul to marry someone?

If so, then Paul would have been in disobedience by choosing to remain single. He chose to remain single most likely because of the nature of his ministry. But if it were God's will for him to marry, then surely he was leaning on his own understanding. If it were God's will for Paul to marry, he should have exercised faith and trusted God to lead him to a good wife and to work out everything else.

3. Is there another option?

So both theories have been ruled out. We cannot say it was God's will for Paul to remain single. We also cannot say it was God's will for Paul to marry. So what then can we say? We could say that God gave Paul leeway and freedom to choose. We could say that Paul exercised wisdom and made what he felt was the best decision. We could say that God's will contained flexibility and that God's purposes for the apostle Paul could have been accomplished either way. I wouldn't go so far as to say that God didn't care one way or the other, but this was not high on God's list on priorities. It was not a major aspect of God's plan that was determined before time, but rather a minor detail over which God was flexible.

The same is true for us. If or whom we marry is not something God stays up at night worrying about. God does not have His fingers crossed hoping that nobody marries Jane before she gets a chance to meet John. God gives us leeway. His will in this regard is not rigid. It is not fixed in stone. It was not predetermined before the foundation of the world. Instead God gives us wisdom to make good choices. That's what we need to pray for – wisdom and guidance. Don't pray for *"the one"* or *"God's perfect will in His perfect timing."* Pray for wisdom to make good choices.

What is God's will for single Christians today?

I can show you even more scriptures where the apostle Paul exercised these principles not only to his own life, but also when giving advice to others. In 1 Corinthians 7, Paul said he wished everyone could remain single like him because the *"time was short."*

Are you loosed from a wife? Do not seek a wife ... (1 Corinthians 7:27)

Then in the book of 1 Timothy, Paul observed that some of the widows in the church were becoming busybodies and getting up to no good. So Paul instructed them to remarry and start a family.

I desire that the younger widows marry ... (1 Timothy 5:14)

So Paul encouraged some people to remain single, and he encouraged others to get married. It all depended on the specific situation. But note that Paul did not instruct the believers to seek God's perfect will whether or not to marry. Rather he taught them *"If you could remain single, remain single. If you can't control yourself, then get married."* These are not the words of a man who believes in God's perfect will in God's perfect timing. Thus we can conclude that the great apostle Paul did not seem to think that God predetermined in advance whether or not we should marry or whom we should marry. He considered it to be a decision based on circumstance rather than design.

Don't take my word for it

I know that this chapter will take a while to digest. But don't take my word for it. Study the scriptures for yourself. I have given you a few scriptures. Check them out. Do your homework and make sure what I am saying is consistent with what the Bible teaches. If you disagree with me, that is perfectly fine. Just make sure your disagreement is based on being true to scripture rather than upholding some tradition you have always believed. What the Bible teaches supersedes what you have always believed.

I believe that we desperately need Bible based teaching on the will of God because there is so much misunderstanding about this topic. Many Christians are trying to build their lives on a misunderstanding of God's will. Many are trying to find a husband or wife based on man-made teachings about the will of God. Don't be one of them. I pray that the truth of scripture will be your guide as you search for a husband or wife.

So based on all I have written in this chapter, how exactly does God guide us into His will? That's what the next chapter is about.

MYTH #3

WAITING TO "HEAR FROM GOD" FIRST

In this chapter

We will learn how God guides us and leads us. We will learn about God's voice and about God's providence. We will learn that obeying Biblical principles, taking heed to godly counsel, and exercising wisdom are more highly valued than a *"word from God."*

Chapter outline

- Oh Dear John
- How God led Philip
- How God leads us
- Wisdom from Proverbs
- Get your GPS on
- God will direct your steps
- More wisdom from Proverbs
- Seems paradoxical?
- Isaac and Rebekah – a story of God's providence
- God's role vs. our role
- Does God choose whom we marry?
- Three *"sort of"* exceptions in the Bible
- Do I need to *"hear from God"*?
- What about prophecies?
- Pray for God's providence

Oh Dear John

A few years ago while I was single, I signed up for a singles seminar. The purpose of this seminar was to teach single Christians how to go about finding a husband or wife. I will confess that the primary reason I signed up was to meet single women. I really was not the least interested in what the host had to say. Let's call him John. He was marketing his book, which I respect, but I was not there for him. Nevertheless there were some things he said that caught my attention.

He was one of those guys who taught single Christians that they should *"wait for God." "God has a perfect will which He will bring to pass in His perfect timing. Be patient."* That was His message. *"If something is God's will, it WILL happen, and nothing could stop it."* He propagated the idea that God will choose your mate because only God knows the person that He ordained for you. Of course we know now that is not how God works.

Then John gave his own testimony how he met and married his wife. Let's call her Elizabeth. When she first met John, she despised him. She hated his guts. She considered him to be way below her standard. But God had spoken to John that Elizabeth would be his wife. So he approached her for the first time and told her *"It is God's will for you to marry me, you need to pray about it."* And he left. I know, you ladies are reading this and swooning. *"Aww, I wish a guy could sweep me off my feet like that."* Elizabeth almost choked on her own vomit. Her first impression was *"Umm No! God has something much better in store for me. MUCH BETTER!"*

But God eventually wore her down. Somebody saw her in the parking lot and asked her, *"Have you considered John yet?"* This person did not even know John. Then the conviction of the Holy Spirit came on her. After a few more experiences like this, she decided to pray, *"Lord is it Your will for me to marry John?"* The Holy Spirit confirmed to her that it was indeed His will. So after much hesitation, she threw her hands up in the air and surrendered to God's perfect will, *"OK Lord not my will but Thine be done."* So with a reluctant heart and a slouching countenance, she dragged herself over to John and said *"Alright, I'll marry you."* She was not thrilled at the time, but she told the gathering that over time she learned to love John and cherish him.

BLAUAUAUAUauaaauuuuuauuuuu

That's the sound of me puking. When I heard that story, I thought to myself, *"What a lousy testimony. God forbid that my wife would have to force herself to love me like that."* Elizabeth practically learned obedience from the things she suffered – being married to John. And this guy was hosting a marriage seminar to teach other Christians how to have that same crappy experience that he called God's perfect will in God's perfect timing. And even more amazingly, all the single ladies were lining up to buy his book. I got absolutely no traction.

Do we have to wait for God to choose our husband or wife? Do we have to be sensitive to hear His voice or else we could end up marrying the wrong person? Is it God's job to choose our mate, or ours? Was John right? Or was he just teaching his subjective understanding of his own experiences? What does the scripture say?

In this chapter, we will look at how God leads us and how to recognize His leading. Here is a revelation for you: you do not need a revelation from God to get married.

How God led Philip

One of the most important things we are called to do on this earth is evangelize – share the gospel with people who are not saved. Look at what happened in Acts 8.

> *Then Philip went down to the city of Samaria and preached Christ to them … Now an angel of the Lord spoke to Philip, saying, "Arise and go toward the south along the road which goes down from Jerusalem to Gaza." … So he arose and went. And behold, a man of Ethiopia, a eunuch of great authority under Candace the queen of the Ethiopians, who had charge of all her treasury, and had come to Jerusalem to worship, was returning. And sitting in his chariot, he was reading Isaiah the prophet. Then the Spirit said to Philip, "Go near and overtake this chariot." … (Acts 8:5, 26-29)*

We see the Holy Spirit giving very specific instructions to Philip and thus led him to preach the gospel to an Ethiopian eunuch. This man, who was very influential in his country, got saved as a result.

Let's pay attention to how the Holy Spirit led Philip. Was Philip sitting at home watching TV when he heard the voice of the Spirit saying *"Philip, go and preach"*? The answer is no. Philip was already preaching in Samaria. While he was doing that, the Spirit spoke to him and gave him specific directions. But Philip did not wait for specific directions before he started preaching. The specific directions only came after. Philip was following the general directions Jesus gave them before He left – *"go into all the world … and be witnesses for Me."*

So let's make a distinction right now between general directions and specific directions. The Holy Spirit gave specific directions to Phillip to preach to a specific person. But Phillip was already following the general directions Jesus had given to preach the gospel and make disciples of all nations (Matthew 28:19; Acts 1:8).

Philip understood a very important principle in being led by the Holy Spirit. Being led by the Spirit does not mean living every minute of every day waiting for specific guidance for every specific situation. *"Lord what should I have for breakfast? Lord should I leave for work now? What about now?"* Seriously, would you want to be married to someone like that? Then don't be someone like that.

Philip understood that he did not need specific guidance for every conceivable situation. He simply needed to follow the general guidelines that God gave us in His Word. And if God wants to give us specific directions, He could. Even that is a big *"if."* There was only one recorded instance where God did this in Philip's life. For the most part, Philip just preached the gospel wherever he had the opportunity, and on rare occasions, God would give him specific guidance where to go.

Also Philip was not waiting for the perfect timing to evangelize. He understood that *"today is the day of salvation"* (2 Corinthians 6:2). He did not wait for any specific guidance to start preaching.

How God leads us

That is a very important principle that we need to understand. The Bible does say we are led by the Spirit (Romans 8:14). But it also says God's Word is a lamp unto our feet and a light unto our path (Psalm 119:105). 99% of the time, we are supposed to simply follow what God's Word says, and if and when God needs to give us specific directions, He will give us. The Holy Spirit works in conjunction with God's Word to guide us.

Many of you are still single because you are waiting for God to tell you whom and when to marry. Some Christians remain in courting relationships for years because one of them is still waiting to *"hear from God."* Instead you should simply follow the principles He has already outlined in His Word for you.

Wisdom from Proverbs

> *Trust in the Lord with all your heart, and lean not on your own understanding; In all your ways acknowledge Him, And He shall direct your paths ... (Proverbs 3:5,6)*

A man's heart plans his way, But the Lord directs his steps ... (Proverbs 16:9)

These scriptures from Proverbs add some more insight into how God directs our steps. We should not lean to our own understanding, but rather trust God. Note that it did not say do not try to understand. The whole book of Proverbs teaches us to *"get understanding."* This verse says whatever understanding we have – don't lean on it. It certainly is not teaching that we need to passively wait for God's directives. We need to acknowledge God in OUR ways – we must plan our way. God uses those plans to direct our steps.

Get your GPS on

Many cars today have a GPS device. Even pedestrians use some kind of GPS app to get around. My wife uses the phone app WAZE. She types in an address or landmark and it gives her directions how to get there. It first plots a road map, and then says *"Begin driving."* WAZE will not say another word until you begin driving. The reason for this is that if you are not moving, the satellite has no way of knowing which direction you are facing. If you start moving in the wrong direction WAZE will instruct you to turn around.

Once it gets you in the right direction, it begins to give further instruction <u>only as you need it</u>. *"In 800 meters, turn left and then turn right."* It reminds you again in 400 meters. WAZE will never tell you *"In 200 meters, keep going straight"* or *"In 10 kilometers, turn left."* It only gives instructions as you need it. If you miss a turn, WAZE then recalibrates. It either instructs you to turn around, or it redirects you to an alternate route. If along the way, WAZE realizes there is traffic up ahead, WAZE may recalibrate and give you another route to bypass the traffic.

My wife uses WAZE all the time. I am personally hesitant to use it … well because … I am a guy. I am a control freak and I don't like to depend on computers. I like to get a mental picture of where WAZE is taking me first before I follow its directions. This makes me comfortable, but if there is a road block or a one-way street or unexpected traffic, then that will throw me off. The satellite is able to see things up ahead that I cannot possibly see.

Sometimes WAZE gives directions that seem counter-intuitive. Just recently, we typed in an address in WAZE in a city with a lot of one-way streets. WAZE said *"turn left"*, when I was certain the place we were going required a right turn. But I decided to trust WAZE for a change. It took us around a big loop, but it helped us to reach our destination without getting lost down a one-way street where we couldn't turn back.

God will direct your steps

This is how God directs our steps. <u>If we are not moving, our steps cannot be directed.</u> We must start moving. Which direction? If we are driving, WAZE does not care which direction you start moving, it will redirect you accordingly. Regarding God's direction and guidance, we must start off just doing what His Word says. Then as we do it, He will give us further direction if we need it and when we need it. The Bible does not say that God will force our steps or walk for us. We have to walk, and as we walk, God directs us.

When it comes to finding a husband or wife, sitting and waiting and hoping and wishing and wondering are not going to get you anywhere. You have to start applying the Biblical principles that God gave to find a husband or wife. As you look, He will then guide you to people you might like, and guide them to you. But He won't do that if you are too passive. You need to be actively looking for good candidates and meeting people. Only then, will God direct your steps to where you need to be.

More wisdom from Proverbs

He who <u>finds</u> a wife finds a good thing ... (Proverbs 18:22)

... a prudent wife is from the Lord ... (Proverbs 19:14)

The Bible tells us that a good wife or prudent wife is from the Lord. But this does not mean that God supernaturally brings a prudent wife to us as we sit passively and wait. The other verse speaks of the man who <u>finds</u> a wife. In order to find, you must seek. So men seek and find a wife AND God gives them a wife at the same time. God works behind the scenes, guiding, and orchestrating things in a way that humans cannot work out.

Seems paradoxical?

Some people think this is a contradiction. On one hand I am saying that YOU should be looking for a mate, but on the other hand GOD directs you to a mate. This is not a contradiction. This is how God works. We need to be acquainted with the God of the Bible.

The Bible tells us that God will supply all our needs according to His riches in glory. Does that mean we should not work? Does that mean we should trust God for supernatural provision like manna in the wilderness? I used to think so. I used to imagine that one day I would walk into my bank and at the end of the transaction I would find an extra million dollars in my account. Then of course, being the honest Christian that I am, I would tell the teller, *"I think there is a mistake here. There seems to be more money in the account than there should be."* Then the teller would say, *"Actually there is no mistake. I remember it distinctly. During the week, someone came and deposited $1 million into your account."* *"Really? Who was it?"* The teller would continue, *"I never got the person's name, but he was wearing a bright white gown and his voice sounded like a choir. And as I turned around to ask his name, he was no longer there. And oh yeah, he had a halo around his head."*

Of course that is pure fantasy. That is not how anything works. The Bible tells us that God gives us the power to get wealth (Deuteronomy 8:18). So that puts everything into perspective. God does supply our needs, but not by giving us wealth. He does so by blessing the work of our hands and causing what we do to prosper. There is no contradiction. God supplies our needs by blessing our work. We work and God supplies – both occur at the same time. No contradiction.

We search for a mate, and God leads us to eligible candidates. No contradiction. If we don't search, God cannot direct us anywhere. Seek and you will find (Matthew 7:7,8). We need to be moving for the GPS to kick in.

Isaac and Rebekah – a story of God's providence

Earlier in this chapter, we saw how God guided Philip while he was preaching in Samaria. Do you know how Philip ended up in Samaria? It is because of God's providence. Read Acts 8.

Providence is a very important word in understanding how God works. God does not micromanage every decision we make and every situation we face. He works providentially. God may occasionally intervene in human affairs, but for the most part He allows us to handle our own business. God prefers to work in the background, quietly working things out for our good. God's providence is best illustrated in the story of Isaac and Rebekah.

Genesis 24 details the beautiful story of how God brought Rebekah to Isaac. Did Isaac sit and wait for God to bring him a wife? It may seem that way, but Isaac actually went searching. In this case, he did not go personally, but his father Abraham sent a servant to get a wife on his behalf. So that was essentially the same thing. Indira and I met on eHarmony. Through my online subscription, eHarmony went on my behalf to match us up, and we took it from there.

I know people who think that God supernaturally and miraculously brought Isaac and Rebekah together. That is simply not true, as we will see. They say that we are not supposed to go looking for our own husband or wife. Instead we are supposed to allow God to bring that person to us. So how do they arrive at this conclusion from Genesis 24? They say that Abraham's servant was a *"type of the Holy Spirit."* Just as the servant brought Rebekah to Isaac, we are to depend on the Holy Spirit to bring our husband or wife to us.

As a Bible teacher, I must explain to you why that interpretation is not correct. There are two ways to interpret Genesis 24. The historical interpretation (physically what happened) and the typological interpretation (you know, that types-and-shadows stuff that preachers like to talk about). The primary historical interpretation is literally what the passage says. Abraham's servant (a human being) went on Abraham's behalf to find a wife (female human being) for Isaac (a male human being). There are no tricks there. It means exactly what it says.

The typological interpretation goes like this. Abraham represented God the Father. The servant represented the Holy Spirit. Isaac represented Christ. Rebekah represented the church. God sent the Holy Spirit on the Day of Pentecost to prepare the church (the bride of Christ) for Christ.

Those are the two possible interpretations of Genesis 24. The interpretation I mentioned earlier is wrong because it mixes up the two. It claims that the servant (a type of the Holy Spirit) will bring a literal husband or wife for us. That is not what this scripture is saying. We need to be clear on that.

If we are not moving, our steps cannot be directed

The servant went on behalf of Isaac to find a wife for him. Abraham simply told the servant where to go (to my home town) to find a wife. All Abraham wanted was a wife from his home town, and not one from Canaan. That was his only condition. As we discussed previously, the servant (who did not know God) prayed for God to send *"the one He appointed for Isaac."* We of course, know now that God did not appoint anyone. But as we read the rest of the chapter, we see God's mighty hand at work providentially.

The servant had no clue where to go or even how to begin finding a wife for Isaac. He just sat by the well with his camels clueless how to proceed. So he prayed for help in the only way he knew how. Even though his prayer was not technically correct, God honored it. Or it might be more accurate to say that God honored Abraham's prayer.

The servant devised a test to determine who would be Isaac's wife. He would ask women to give him water, and whichever one gave water to him and his camels, that was the one. DO NOT try this at home. Do not go about looking for a husband or wife that way. This servant did this because he did not know what else to do. By the end of this book, you will know better. Nevertheless that was how he did it.

Then Rebekah came by and did exactly as the servant had prayed. Not only that, she was from Abraham's family line, she was beautiful, and she was a virgin. After he spoke to Rebekah's family and told them the story, it was crystal clear to them that God was orchestrating all of this. They could only marvel and say,

> *"The thing comes from the Lord; we cannot speak to you either bad or good. Here is Rebekah before you; take her and go, and let her be your master's son's wife, as the Lord has spoken." ... (Genesis 24:50-51)*

It was clear to all that God was providentially orchestrating everything. Rebekah was a good wife who came from the Lord. But no one was passive in this entire process. Abraham and Isaac sent a servant in proxy to look for a wife (with God's guidance of course). The servant had to find someone. Then Rebekah had to choose to leave her father's house and go with the servant to Isaac. A lot of things needed to happen to make that match. And every step of the way, God was in the background providentially guiding and working it out.

The point I am trying to make is that the human agents were not passive while God micromanaged everything. But rather, they all did their part, and God worked providentially to bring it to pass. <u>God does not micromanage, He guides. He does not dictate, He directs</u>. As we make the effort to do what we have to do, God blesses it and prospers our way.

Please do not think it is our job to sit and wait and hope while God miraculously brings someone to us. That is not how it works. We need to know the difference between providentially and supernaturally. As you make the effort to meet people and make yourself known to members of the opposite sex, God will work providentially and guide you to eligible candidates from which you can choose.

God's role vs. our role

With most things, there is a part that God has to play, and there is a part that we have to play. When you need a job, do you sit at home and wait for an employer to call you? You have to work on your résumé and send in applications – give God something to work with.

The same is true with finding a husband or wife. God is not going to miraculously bring someone to you. Unless your name is Sleeping Beauty, God is not going to send a prince to cut through a forest of thorns to get to you. Get rid of the thorns and baggage in your own life first. Wake up and do something. God will providentially send the right people in and out of your life as you do your part – work on yourself, meet people and make yourself known. Get friends to introduce you to other single people. If there are no single members of the opposite sex in your church, visit other churches. Visit other churches anyway to keep your options open. As you do what you can do, trust God to lead you and to direct your steps to the person who is best for you. We will talk much more later on about proactive things you can do.

Does God choose whom we marry?

I have been running the bibleissues.org website for over 15 years. One of the most frequent Google search phrases that lead people to my site is some variation of *"Does God choose my husband?"* These folks are interested in knowing if their husband or wife is someone that God chooses for them (perhaps before the foundation of the world), or someone they must choose.

Based on everything I have written so far, it is clear what I believe. And not just believe, I am convinced of it from scripture. It is OUR job to choose whom we marry. It is not God's job. God's job is to guide and to lead. He gives us wisdom, and then gives us freedom to make our decisions. It is our job to choose. God instructs Christians to marry Christians of the opposite gender. Then we determine what other qualities we want, and we look for potential candidates who fit that description, and ultimately we choose whom we marry. God guides the overall process just as He guided Abraham's servant in Genesis 24. God may also guide us NOT to marry certain persons. We will deal with this later on.

God is in control but He does not micromanage. God is active in the entire process, but He is not a control freak. Tell me which of the following people is really in control.

BOSS #1:

He bosses around everyone and rules with an iron fist, causing his employees to obey him out of fear. The employees hate him and constantly grumble behind his back, but they do their job because they don't want to get fired.

BOSS #2:

He motivates and inspires his employees to reach their full potential and to achieve personal satisfaction in their job. He creates a very safe working environment that makes it conducive for his employees to do their best.

Both of them get their employees to work, but boss #2 is truly in control. God is in control, but He is not a control freak. He equips us with wisdom, He gives us freedom to choose, and He guides us providentially in our search for a mate. That is how God works.

Three "*sort of*" exceptions in the Bible

As we noted earlier, the Bible uses terminology like *"Abraham took a wife."* This terminology strongly implies that it was Abraham who made his own choice, and not God who chose a wife for Abraham before the foundation of the world. That's how it worked in most cases. That's the default.

There are a few instances in the Bible when it APPEARS as though God worked differently. People use these scriptures to teach that God chooses whom we marry, and therefore we should not marry unless we *"hear from God."* But as we shall see, appearances can be deceiving.

Adam and Eve

Then the rib which the Lord God had taken from man He made into a woman, and <u>He brought her to the man</u> ... (Genesis 2:22)

There are folks who use this verse to tell you that it is God's job to bring your wife to you ... just as He brought Eve to Adam.

If they don't realize that Adam and Eve's situation was kinda different from yours and mine, I don't know what to say. It is true that God created Eve and brought her to Adam. Yes that is true. But you could just as easily say that God caused all the women in the world to parade naked before Adam, and then told him to pick one. That would also accurately describe what happened in the Garden of Eden. There was only one woman on the earth. It was not rocket science. Adam did not need to pray and fast to determine who was God's perfect will for him. Their situation was clearly unique.

Hosea and Gomer

> ... *the Lord said to Hosea: "Go, take yourself a wife of harlotry" ... So he went and <u>took Gomer</u> the daughter of Diblaim, and she conceived and bore him a son ... (Hosea 1:2-3)*

God told the prophet Hosea to marry a harlot. Then according to verse 3, he married Gomer. God never told him to marry Gomer specifically. All God told Hosea was to take a wife from among the harlots. Hosea chose Gomer. This was his choice. He should have known from her name alone that she was nothing but trouble.☺

Now the reason God meddled in Hosea's life is because God had specifically called him to be a living-example prophet. His life would be a prophecy of how Israel committed adultery against God, and how God loved them unconditionally, and purchased their redemption. So God had a specific purpose for telling Hosea to marry a harlot – a purpose that was unique to Hosea. But even so, God still did not choose a wife for Hosea. He still gave Hosea a choice.

Joseph and Mary

Joseph was betrothed to Mary, but she came home one day pregnant. Joseph wanted none of it. He was thinking about putting her away privately. But,

> ... *an angel of the Lord appeared to him in a dream, saying, "Joseph, son of David, do not be afraid to take to you Mary your wife, for that which is conceived in her is of the Holy Spirit" ... (Matthew 1:20)*

It appears that God is telling Joseph whom to marry, but we must remember that Joseph was already betrothed to Mary. They had already met. They were already in a relationship. God was not telling Joseph to marry a complete stranger who was God's perfect will for him. God was simply telling Joseph to go ahead with the plans they had already made. And of course, the reason for this was that they had the unique situation where they were about to give birth to the incarnate Christ. I believe that the only reason God wanted this specific match is because both Joseph and Mary were from the tribe of Judah.

So we see three examples in scripture where God appeared to intervene and direct people whom to marry – Adam and Eve, Hosea and Gomer, Joseph and Mary. Every single one of those had some element of uniqueness. Do you believe that your marriage is intricately intertwined in God's plan of redemption? If not, then don't expect God to intervene and tell you whom to marry. God is going to leave that up to you. What He will do is give you wisdom and providentially bring people in and out of your life. You do your part, and let God do His.

In just about everything in life, God leads us and guides us without overriding our free will. He gives us wisdom and guides us providentially, but ultimately we must exercise wisdom and discretion and make decisions for ourselves. We must apply the principles outlined in God's Word, together with the leading of the Holy Spirit, together with wisdom to make good choices.

Do I need to "hear from God"?

Many of us think that being led by the Spirit means that we must hear the *"voice of God"* or get a *"word from God."* Jesus said that the Holy Spirit will lead us into truth (John 16:13) … Your Word is truth (John 17:17). The Bible also says that God's Word is a lamp unto our feet, a light unto our path (Psalm 119:105). The Holy Spirit uses whatever understanding we have of the Word of God to guide us. If we don't understand the basic principles of God's Word, we have given the Holy Spirit very little to work with.

Many Christians find themselves in that situation, and therefore are unable to follow the leading of the Spirit in their lives. For this reason, they will flock to *"prophets"* who will tell them what God is saying. Or they will claim to hear the voice of God directly. Rather than making plans for their lives and being diligent like the ant (Proverbs 6:6-8), they just wait for God to speak to them. I have learned from experience that very often when someone says *"Thus saith the Lord"*, God did not actually speak to them. They are simply telling you the thoughts that came into their mind – assuming that those thoughts are God's thoughts. And they call it the voice of God.

Michael was attracted to Nancy, but Nancy did not feel the same way. He walked up to Nancy one day in church and said to her *"God told me to sit next to you."* Nancy's mother sensing her discomfort, leaned over and said to Michael *"Well God told me that seat is reserved for my sister."* Clearly they didn't both hear from God.

Now let me make it very clear that God can and does speak to us. He speaks mainly through His Word. If you have God's Word in your heart, then God can and will put thoughts into your mind when you need it.

I recall an occasion about 20 years ago, I was getting dressed to collect my mom from work. My mother worked in the psychiatric unit of the local hospital (AKA the mad house☺). I specifically felt that God wanted me to wear a white T-shirt and black pants, so I did. When I got to the hospital, my mother asked me to pray with a patient who had not been responding to anyone for the past 2 weeks. When I approached her, I realized that we were wearing the same outfit. I noticed her looking at my clothing, then hers, then mine, then hers, repeatedly. I realized that in her mind, she was identifying with the fact that we were wearing the same clothing. To the amazement of the nurses, she spoke briefly with me that evening and I was able to make progress with her through subsequent visits.

That day God gave me specific instructions what to wear. Does that mean that I should seek God on a daily basis about my clothing choices? No! He has given certain instructions how to dress. I just need to stay within those boundaries, and if God wants me to wear something specific, He will let me know.

We must resist the temptation to think that every thought that comes into our mind is a *"word from God."* I know of one pastor who constantly told his congregation what *"God told him."* When they questioned how he knew it was God speaking to him and not his own thoughts, he told them that he was praying and fasting for 3 days when those thoughts came to him. That's how he knew it was God speaking. Well apparently this pastor is greater than Jesus Himself. Jesus was fasting for 40 days and the next voice he heard was the voice of the devil. Jesus responded to the devil with the words, *"It is written ..."* This clearly suggests that what is written is far more important than any voice you hear.

~~~~~~

God does not micromanage, He guides.
He does not dictate, He directs

~~~~~~

A few years ago I taught classes in my church Bible School, and one of the students came to me with a vision she had. She had a vision where she heard God promise her that He would send a rich Christian business man to be her husband. She wanted my feedback on it. So I asked my student,

> *Why is it that when God speaks to people nowadays, He always tells them exactly what they want to hear? In the Bible days, God very often told people the exact opposite of what they wanted to hear. Has God changed? If God has*

a reputation for telling people what they don't want to hear, and you have a voice telling you exactly what you want to hear, then isn't it likely that the voice you are hearing is your own mind playing tricks on you? Why is God's will for you to marry a rich businessman? Why not a poor construction worker? Why not a struggling pastor?

Further, what was the point of the vision? Most likely, it would only succeed in causing her to reject any potential husband who was not a rich businessman. I haven't followed up with my student to know what happened to her. Did she marry a Christian business man? Did she marry someone else? Is she still waiting? I don't know. But whether or not she got lucky does not change the principles clearly outlined in scripture. Don't follow voices. We are supposed to test every spirit. Follow Biblical principles.

There are more sure ways God can communicate with us without giving us a revelation. If you don't feel a peace in your spirit about a relationship you're in, that could be a red flag. We'll talk more about this in Myth #7.

What about prophecies?

Many people have been led astray and have made very bad decisions because of voices and words and prophecies. If you are single and reading this, I am almost certain that you have had at least one prophet tell you that *"God is preparing someone really special for you"* or something to that effect. If you don't know better, that will fill your eyes with tears and your heart with hope. There is of course nothing wrong with having hope. It's just that hope should be based on a definite promise of God, and not the ranting of some prophet. You need Biblical hope, not false hope.

A prophet came to a church one day and pulled out a woman saying that she would soon be married to an engineer. This shocked her and all the members seeing that she was already married and her husband was not an engineer. When the prophet learned this, instead of admitting he was wrong, he insisted that God would work it out anyway, but he wasn't sure how. 15 years later, she is still married to her husband, who is still not an engineer.

My wife, Indira had a number of those prophecies when she was single. If those prophets are all to be believed, then I am supposed to be tall and thin, short and fat, all at the same time. One prophet told her that her husband would be tall and thin, another said he would be stocky. I really hope this doesn't mean I will end up gaining weight and losing height.

Another prophet said her husband would love and cherish her. That last one turned out to be right.

But how do you know which prophet is right? Here is my advice. Whenever a prophet comes to you with a word, assume that the word is not from God. Let him prove otherwise. In the Old Testament, prophets actually had to give a sign to prove that they were from God. Many modern-day *"prophets"* are not actually hearing from God. Many of them are predators just looking to prey on people who are vulnerable. They know that single people who are searching are usually very anxious about getting married, and will grasp on to anyone who promised them something good. Some may genuinely have a word from God. Others may turn out to be right purely by luck.

Here are some things you can look out for whenever you get a prophecy. Does this word confirm what you already believe God has been telling you? Is this a word in season that uplifts you just when you needed it the most? Did the prophecy come from someone whom you know is operating in the fruit of love? By their fruits you will know them (Matthew 7:15,16). Did the prophecy or word come from someone whom you trust? Do you know that the Bible (especially the book of Proverbs) has a lot more to say about listening to wise counselors than to prophets?

> *Where there is no counsel, the people fall; But in the multitude of counselors there is safety ... (Proverbs 11:14)*

Kathy *"heard from God"* that she and Mark would be married on a specific date. At the time, Mark was in a live-in relationship with a woman with whom he had a child. He had no relationship whatsoever with Kathy. But her faith was strong. Nothing could shake her faith. She claimed that whenever she would doubt God, God would order her steps in such a way that she and Mark would always end up in the same place at the same time. They did not engage in long conversations, but he would wave or say a brief hello, and this was enough to restore her faith in her *"word from God."* She convinced her two best friends that this was from God. They even looked up to her as an example of faith being the evidence of things not seen – a strong woman who believed against the odds.

As the day approached, she excitedly got prepared. Even though she still did not have a relationship with Mark, she started to plan a wedding. She purchased a wedding dress and all the accessories. On the day, she sat in a church fully dressed for her wedding. She had even convinced a pastor to believe in her word from God, and he was there on that day in a fully decorated church to perform the ceremony.

The day came, she waited in the church, but Mark never showed. This was not hard to believe since he did not even know about the wedding. She was crushed and has never quite recovered from the disappointment. That was over 20 years ago and Mark is still in a relationship with the mother of his child. Kathy blamed all the others around her who did not have faith. She still believed God would have done it, but she needed to be quiet and not allow others to steal her faith. Don't be like Kathy.

Pray for God's providence

Indira and I met on eHarmony. How I ended up on eHarmony is actually an example of God's providence. A cousin of mine told me that one of her friends met her husband on eHarmony. That very night, I signed up for a one-year subscription. Not too long after, I excitedly told my cousin that I joined eHarmony. She then told me that she had made a mistake. It wasn't eHarmony her friend used, it was some other dating site that I don't remember now. But within this 12 month period, Indira and I were matched up on eHarmony and the rest is history.

Did God tell me to join eHarmony? Nope. But did He guide me to eHarmony? Absolutely. God even used misinformation to lead me to that particular dating site. This is an example of God working providentially to cause things to work out for our good.

Pray for God to work providentially in your own life. Pray for God to bring people into your life, take people out of your life, and to bring you into other people's lives. Ask God to open the right doors and close the wrong doors. Ask God to lead you to the right places. Then ask God for wisdom so you can make the best choice.

MYTH #4

WAITING FOR GOD TO "WORK IT OUT"

In this chapter

We will learn about the dangers of being too passive in our walk with God. We will discuss a number of proactive things Christians can do to help find a marriage partner, and how to prepare yourself while you are searching.

Chapter outline

- Passivity
- Dangers of passivity
- Not even Ruth *"waited"* for Boaz
- Did Joshua really kiss dating goodbye?
- *"Dating"* is important
- Marriage requires work
- Proactive things Christians can do to help find a mate
- Prepare yourself

Passivity

There are people who make things happen
There are people who wait for things to happen
And there are people who wonder what happened

Indira and I met online, and we knew immediately we had found what we were looking for. But we know others who do not believe that Christians should meet online. In fact, we know Christians who are waiting for us to get divorced so they could say *"I told you so."* These people absolutely insist that God must bring your spouse to you while you do absolutely nothing. This is what I refer to as passivity – the belief that we must wait for or depend on God to do everything. As we have seen in the earlier chapters, faith is not passive. Faith is active. Faith without works is dead.

A passive Christian says *"God will work it out"* while they fail or refuse to do what they are supposed to do. A passive Christian misunderstands the balance between trusting God and taking initiative. These Christians adopt a passive approach to searching for a spouse, and even after they get married, they adopt a passive approach to handling problems that arise in the marriage. A passive Christian takes a *"wait and see"* approach to life. The Bible never calls us to *"wait and see what happens."* The Bible teaches us to put action to our faith – in other words, make things happen.

The reason Christians tend to believe this myth is because they have been taught that if it is God's will for two people to be together, it will happen and nothing could stop it. Of course, we know now that this is a gross misunderstanding of God's will. We have already seen that God's will does not work that way.

Dangers of passivity

There was a couple who met in high school and dated for 8 years before they finally decided to get married. Having finally gotten married after dating for so long, they proceeded to get divorced 10 months later. How do you get divorced so quickly after being together for so long?

A non-Christian friend of mine has a theory on how this whole debacle could have been avoided. He believes every couple should live together first for a few years before they get married. That way, they will know before they get married whether they could actually live with each other. As far as

Hollywood and the world are concerned, this is just the way it is nowadays. Note that this is my friend's reasoning, not mine.

Here is the major flaw in his reasoning. He is assuming that if two people are right for each other, their marriage will *"just work out."* He believes it is either they can live together or they can't. That fact is set in stone, and the only way to know for sure is to actually live together and see what happens. This is a very passive mentality.

The fact is that people can learn to live with each other. People can learn to make themselves easier to live with. Most of us grew up with brothers and sisters who were not always easy to live with. But we won't rate our childhood as being unhappy because of it.

Think about that. We have grown up with brothers and sisters and even though they annoyed and irritated us at times, we never had the option of divorcing them. We had no choice but to stick it out. Why is it that people are so quick to pull the divorce trigger when marital problems arise? We do have the ability to make a relationship work if we develop the right mindset.

~~~~~~

She didn't really know what she wanted until she started working on herself

~~~~~~

Here is something else to think about. When last have you heard of a parent divorcing their child? I have seen parents put up with the most deviant behavior from their kids. They sacrifice their entire life and happiness for the sake of their children. They take them from school to soccer practice, they do their homework for them, clean up their rooms, feed them. In return, the kids show nothing but ingratitude. When they are teenagers, they are ashamed to be seen with their parents in public. Yet the parents gladly suck it up and do whatever it takes to make their kids happy. If husbands and wives showed half of that devotion to each other, do you think the divorce rate would be over 50%?

The fact is that people do have the ability to make a relationship work. They just apply those skills to every relationship other than the husband / wife relationship. They go all out for their kids, their parents, their siblings and even their friends. But not for their spouses. Why is that?

It is simply not true that if two people are right for each other, they will automatically be able to live with each other. Nothing like that is ever automatic. You need to take whatever compatibility you have, and then add to it a lot of work. Compatibility does not negate the need for hard work. It is a myth to believe that if two people are compatible, their marriage will *"just work out."* Nothing will just work out on its own while we adopt a passive approach. If our marriage is going to work out, we must work it out.

The truth is that people don't get divorced because they are non-Christians. The divorce rate among Christians is more or less the same as non-Christians. People get divorced because they don't work on their marriage.

A passive attitude rears its ugly head in two ways. Firstly, single people who are not yet married tend to be way too passive in their search for Mr. or Ms. Right. They are usually not proactive enough, and they either get lucky or they meet someone later in life. Secondly, after they finally get married, they tend to be passive in handling issues that come up in the marriage. They expect God to work everything out because they are both Christians. As a result, major problems go unresolved in their marriage while they are trusting God to *"work it out."* This myth is primarily responsible for the passive attitude many Christians adopt when they actually do get into a relationship and marriage. They assume that because their marriage is God's will, it has to work. The truth is that if they don't work at it, it may end up not working out.

Bottom line: passivity is a killer both in finding a husband or wife, and in developing a happy marriage.

Not even Ruth *"waited"* for Boaz

The story of Ruth and Boaz is considered to be one of the most epic love stories in the Bible, and a great pattern for single Christians to emulate. In fact, the concept of *"waiting for your Boaz"* is very popular among authors and preachers. But if you actually read this scripture, you will see that not even Ruth waited for Boaz.

> *Then Naomi her mother-in-law said to her "... wash yourself and anoint yourself, put on your best garment and go down to the threshing floor; but do not make yourself known to the man until he has finished eating and drinking. Then it shall be, when he lies down, that you shall notice the place where he lies; and you shall go in, uncover his feet, and lie down; and he will tell you what you should do."*
>
> *... So she went down to the threshing floor and did according to all that her mother-in-law instructed her.*
>
> *And after Boaz had eaten and drunk, and his heart was cheerful, he went to lie down at the end of the heap of grain; and she came softly, uncovered his feet, and lay down. Now it happened at midnight that the man was startled, and turned himself; and there, a woman was lying at his feet. And he said, "Who are you?"*

So she answered, "I am Ruth, your maidservant. Take your maidservant under your wing, for you are a close relative."

... *Ruth 3:1-9*

I know this is a weird portion of scripture. I find it hilarious at times when pastors are preaching from this passage, and they speak with such passion about how Ruth took a step of faith, and Boaz agreed to redeem her. You could sense the excitement building to a boiling point, then shouts of *"AMEN"* burst out from the crowd followed by tears of joy. People get up off their feet with hands raised to the heavens thanking and praising God. And I am sitting there thinking, *"Gross! Weren't they, like, related to each other?"*

Admittedly, what makes this story great is not the crazy culture and customs they had. It is the fact that this story foreshadowed Christ's redemption of us. So that part of it is totally not gross.

Let's take away the main point. Ruth did not sit in Naomi's house waiting for her prince to show up. Imagine that. Not even Ruth was *"waiting for her Boaz."* She did something. She took matters into her own hands. She had her mother-in-law coach her as she take a great step of faith. And through her proactivity, God worked it out. It did not *"just work out."* She did her part, then God did His part, and it worked out.

It is important that we get the correct take away from this. You need to do something – perhaps not sleep by some guy's foot for him to marry you – but something. If you are like most Christians, you probably need to be a little more proactive than you presently are.

Did Joshua really kiss dating goodbye?

There is a popular book called *"I kissed dating goodbye"* written by Joshua Harris. This is a great book, and I strongly recommend it. It contains some very good principles that single Christians should take heed to.

However, the title of the book is misleading. It gives the impression that Christians should not date, and therefore the only way to find a husband or wife is for God to do all the work; and that God must bring this person into your life without you dating. That is actually NOT what Joshua Harris' book is about. Yet many single Christians have used that book to come to the wrong conclusion that they must passively wait for God to bring them a husband or wife.

I know enough about publishing to know that that title was chosen primarily because it was catchy. But the title does not adequately describe what the book is really about. The basic idea of that book is that Christians should not date UNTIL they are ready for marriage. They should desist from the practice of CASUAL DATING. That is, dating and being alone and intimate with members of the opposite sex in a relationship that is leading nowhere other than to fornication. That is what Mr. Harris' book is about.

In his follow-up book, *"Boy meets girl"* – a much less catchy title – he describes how he met Shannon. During their courtship, they went on dates. But by then, he was ready for marriage. That's the difference.

Don't come to the wrong conclusion that you should be completely passive while God miraculously brings someone to you. God will bring people in and out of your lives, just as He will bring you in and out of people's lives. When it comes to finding a mate, don't adopt a passive approach. You need to be a little proactive without being overly aggressive or too passive. That balance is what you need to find.

"Dating" is important

Christian dating can give us the opportunity to understand ourselves and how we interact with the opposite sex as we grow and develop. It gives us the knowledge we need to choose someone who is good for us.

Now of course we must exercise wisdom in dating. Dating should not include sexual intimacy. Dating should be done in a manner so as to not compromise your Christian walk or testimony. Group settings and situations that do not lead us into temptation are important. Also, avoid deep commitments too early in life. Keep it light and social, and focus on having as many friends as possible – of both sexes.

Amanda was a pastor's daughter. She grew up in a sheltered home. Her father did not believe that teenage girls should socialize with young men. She therefore did not have close male friends growing up. In her early 20s, she married a church boy called Raymond, who turned out to be rotten to the core. He eventually left her for another woman.

Now in her late 30s, Amanda has realized that she does not know what she likes in a man. She does not know what she does not like in a man. She has never had the opportunity to get to know members of the opposite sex in a controlled setting. It's no wonder that she married the first guy that came along. It is important to have as many Christian friends as possible of both genders and not close the door too soon.

Marriage requires work

Passivity also rears its ugly head after people get married. Passive Christians believe that God will miraculously bring their husband and wife to them. These folks are also likely to believe that God will miraculously make their marriage work without much effort on their part.

Kimberly insists that her marriage to Randy was *"God's will"* since it was God who brought them together. During their courtship, Randy was unhappy with the closeness of male friends Kimberly had, so he took a break from the relationship. But Kimberly was not worried. She was convinced it was *"God's will"*, so she did nothing but wait for Randy to come back to her, which he did.

She took this same passive attitude into the marriage. During difficult times, she reassured herself that the marriage was God's doing from the beginning, and He would work it out. If God ordained that marriage before the foundation of the world and brought them together in the *"fullness of time"*, then according to her logic, God would work out any other problem that comes up. This was God's will, nothing could stand in its way.

The problem is that Kimberly is a very difficult person to live with, and no one – not even God – could convince her that she is anything less than perfect. She berates her husband in public, and he meekly tucks his tail between his legs. She does not feel the need to grow or to change her ways, *"God will work it out."* It never occurred to her that the only reason her marriage is working is because her husband is submissive. He is not happy.

If she would realize that she has a part to play, and not just *"leave it to God"*, then she would have a much happier marriage. It is one thing to not get divorced. It is another thing to be happily married. Kimberly's problem is her passive attitude.

Proactive things Christians can do to help find a mate

OK, so far I have given you a lot of theory. Now let's get down to business. What are some of the proactive things you can do to increase your chances of finding a good Christian husband or wife? Notice my terminology. I did not say God's perfect match, because you are not looking for a specific person.

When Isaac was of age, Abraham sought to find a wife for him. He was sure that he wanted that wife to be from his hometown and not from Canaan. Therefore he sent his servant to … his hometown. Basically, you should do whatever is humanly possible to place yourself where eligible members of the opposite sex are. What kind of person are you looking for?

What kind of person is that person looking for? Where are those people found? That's where you need to be.

Visit other churches

Christians go to church. If you are a single woman looking for a husband, there is a chance that you go to a church where there aren't a lot of Christian men. Just remember that there are other churches. Hopefully your youth group should be well networked with other churches. If not, you can visit other churches informally. It is better to visit other churches in a group rather than individually. The reason for this is that if you go alone, depending on how socially outgoing you are, you might find it very difficult to actually meet other eligible singles. If you don't have an active singles group in your church, get a couple of single friends to go with you. And don't take blockers with you – you know the people who will prevent you from meeting other singles. Leave them at home.

When you visit, you main interest should be in meeting people. Remember, you are not looking for *"the one."* Get to know as many people as you could. Use social media to remain in contact after you leave. This way you can arrange to meet casually at a later time. Meeting in groups is always safe. The more eligible singles you meet, the better your chances of finding what you are looking for. Give God's providence a chance to work.

Get involved in ministry

More than just visiting churches, it is important to get involved in ministries. I am not saying that you need to be in ministry for God to send someone to you. I am saying that when you are involved in ministry, you get better interaction with other like-minded Christians. If you are a university student, get involved in Intervarsity, Campus Crusade, or whatever other Christian groups are available at your school. The best-case scenario is to meet your husband or wife in university and marry not too long after you graduate.

Here is a testimony from Stephanie (a member of our Bible Issues Facebook group):

> *I met my husband, Garett, at Bible school in our early 20s. We were friends and "just part of the group" for the first half. Then we and some others started to pray together for funds for the year-end mission trip. We could tell something was happening between us, but didn't tell each other. Something that really attracted me to him was that he loved the Lord and was passionate about the truth. He played guitar and loved to worship.*
>
> *I prayed to God to take the feelings away. I was at a point where I had surrendered guys to God and didn't want another in my life. I had seen God*

shut the door with two others during this time. However, the door wasn't shutting with Garett.

Our class went to Grenada for a month. We spent any time we could together: ministry, and hanging out. At one point a married couple asked to pray for us as they had appreciated people praying for them before they got married. We weren't even going out at the time. That night we confessed our attraction to each other and we were a couple afterward.

How did I know he was what I was looking for? God didn't shut the door as He did with others; he respected me (our first kiss was on the cheek after a month of going out). I had a peace. We have been married for 25 years in May [2018], have 4 children, and are missionaries in Mexico. God is good!

They were both in Bible School and a missionary ministry, which gave them the opportunity to meet and to interact. Also interestingly, Stephanie did not pray for it to work out, but for it not to work out. The one time God did not answer that prayer, she took it as a positive sign. That's faith.

Get friends to introduce you

39% of people meet their significant other through friends in common. Another 18% meet through work. Only 22% meet in social settings and 15% online. So you are more likely to find your husband or wife through friends, family and associates; than on your own. Even Abraham used someone he knew to help find a wife for Isaac.

Sharon was unmarried and getting on in age. Her sister Betty was anxious to find her a husband. She would look around everywhere she went. One day she went to do her hair and while there she asked the hair dresser if she knew anyone for her sister. It turned out that she did. Betty's hairdresser arranged for Sharon to meet her guy. Things worked out and today they are happily married. Sharon has never been more self-confident and successful.

Do not be ashamed to do the same thing. We all have friends and family. Let them be part of your search. Trust me they will be glad to help. People are inherently meddlesome. Use that to your advantage. Get friends and family and even coworkers to introduce you to eligible bachelors and bachelorettes. One of the principles I lived by when I was single was that you have absolutely nothing to lose by meeting people.

While Indira was single, she had another single Christian friend who nagged her incessantly to join eHarmony. Very reluctantly, she did. It took a while, but eventually eHarmony matched her up with this amazing guy☺ who they calculated to be 99% compatible with her, and they later got married.

William and Maryke (two members of our Bible Issues Facebook group) met through common friends. Their testimony is as follows:

I met my husband at a restaurant. He was actually a friend of a friend from a Bible group. He asked for my number a week after that and we started chatting. After five months we both knew our search was over. It was just the fact that I knew this guy would walk in front of a bus for me. We got married after five months. Both of us were the type of people who would walk away from struggles and hardships, but we worked through it because we made that promise in front of God. I think I can thank God daily because if we did not have the Holy Spirit to guide us, we would have given up on each other a long time ago. Now almost six years later we are very much in love. And we both know marriage is not just a fairytale, it's hard work and constant love.

Try online dating

Even though only 15% of people meet their husband or wife online, it is not a small number. There are lots of online dating sites / apps at your disposal. You have absolutely nothing to lose by trying them.

I have a personal bias toward eHarmony because that's how Indira and I met. What I like about eHarmony is that you don't have to sift through profiles as in other sites. The problem with profiles is that people put their best picture and write the best thing about themselves. You are more likely to meet the person who is best at marketing themselves rather than the person who is best for you. eHarmony has a proprietary compatibility matching software, and they provide the matches for you. That was perfect for busy people like Indira and me. And most importantly, it worked for us.

If however, you prefer to sift through other people's profiles, that is fine. Match, Our Time, Christian Mingle, and others are also great. Just a word about Christian Mingle. Christians should be looking for other Christians to marry. But there is no rule that says you need a Christian dating site. Almost all matchmaking sites give you the option to filter search results by religion. Christian Mingle further allows you to filter by denomination. But you can find Christians on other dating sites. And also, there is nothing preventing people from setting up fake-profiles. So with every dating site, please exercise caution. Do not give out important information. And make sure your first meeting is in a safe public place.

Again, this is another advantage of eHarmony. It takes you through phases so that you get to progressively learn more about the other person through guided interaction, before moving on to personal email and phone calls. This gives you sufficient time to weed out the crazies and those you are not interested in.

James (a member of our Bible Issues Facebook group) also met his wife online.

I met my wife online through a website called Christiancafe.com. I was 37 or 38 at the time. I was never married before, went out with some girls but usually the ones I liked just wanted me to be in the friend zone, which is all good. It did bother me somewhat that I was getting older as I wanted to get married and have children. That was pretty much the desire of my heart, a family.

But through waiting and some heartaches, I met the most wonderful lady. Neneng is from the Philippines and sent me a message on the website. At first I wasn't sure about this, she was 10,000 miles away, and I didn't want a long distance relationship. However, after talking with her on-line and over the phone there was something about her.

After two weeks I felt comfortable in my spirit and felt I wanted to marry her and I asked her if she would. She said yes even though she had doubts – she said because I had not seen her in person, only in pictures. Well I just knew she was a godly woman and someone who loved family and children and was beautiful.

So I went to visit her in the Philippines so we could start the fiancé visa process. It's kind of funny when I got there because at that time when you arrive in Manila and leave the airport you cross the road to meet the person in a big waiting area. So here I am going through this looking for this petit 4' 10" girl and everyone is staring at me. I finally found her. She was even more beautiful in person and such a kind spirit. She remained pure for the Lord because she was a godly woman.

When driving home from the airport though I noticed she was real quiet and not very talkative. We got to her house where she lived with her sisters and a cousin and they put me in the one room with air conditioning (thank goodness) and she slept in one of the other rooms. I was a little worried because she was so quiet. Then that morning she brought me warm tea and breakfast and her whole disposition was changed. She told me later on that at first she wasn't sure about marrying this big American. She was praying that night and she felt a calm in her spirit like God was saying "You have been praying for a husband, now here is a fellow believer so what's the problem?"

So for three weeks we had a wonderful time. As soon as I got back to the US, I filled out the visa paperwork and 10 months later she got her fiancé visa. I scheduled a date at the courthouse to get married the day after she arrived. When she got here I asked her if she wanted to plan a wedding at my church or get married at the courthouse. She said she wanted to get married the next day as she would not live together without getting married or she would live with her twin sister in Tennessee until we got married. Needless to say we got married the next day.

She is more than I ever hoped for, a godly, caring, loving wife and mother who has made my life complete. So at 39 I got married, good things come to those that wait.

As a testimony after we got married, we had been trying for over a year to get pregnant but nothing. I went to the doctor and after the test he said the problem was with me and all my swimmers were dead (don't know how else to explain that). I went to my pastor with tears, I was heartbroken. We talked and he said, "Hey let's give God a chance." So that Sunday he prayed for me in church and that week my wife got pregnant. We have two wonderful boys now. Glory to God!

Should women make the first move?

This is entirely up to you. There is no rule regarding who should make the first move. It has nothing to do with headship. It is solely a matter of personal preference.

Most women prefer men to make the first move. But if there is one thing you learn from this book, don't be passive. Don't sit and wait and hope for something to happen. You may not wish to make the first move, but you can still give some non-verbal cue that you are interested and that you are approachable. This would make it easy for the guy to make the first move.

Other women don't mind taking the initiative. Ruth was proactive. My only advice is to not be too pushy. You would only come across as desperate. In the early stages of a relationship, there are a lot of two-way exchanges. If the other person is not responding, then they are not worth chasing.

Prepare yourself

Marcy met her husband-to-be in college, although at the time, she was not at all attracted to him. She saw him as a big brother. He treated her well, he was the stereotypical nice guy, but that was not what she was looking for at the time. They both went their separate ways after college. It would be another 14 years before they would meet again.

During this time, Marcy got proactive in preparing herself for marriage. Her pastor counseled her to work on herself so that when she met the person she would marry, that person would reciprocate. She did a lot of work on her personality, physique, and emotional stability. As she grew, she found her desires and preferences changing. She started working on a list of what she wanted in a husband, and she found her mind wandering back to college – she wanted someone who treated her just as well as her *"friend"* from college. Soon after, God providentially arranged for their paths to cross again, and the rest is history.

What was interesting about her story is that she didn't really know what she wanted until she started working on herself. Being ready for marriage has nothing to do with age, but maturity. You may be looking for someone, but how do you know that person is also looking for you? It may be in your best interest to do some work on yourself before looking for someone to marry. Here are some of the ways you can work on yourself.

Get rid of emotional baggage

One of the major pitfalls of modern dating is dating dictated by emotional baggage. Open your suitcase, we all have one. What do you find in your emotional bag? Daddy issues? Were you sexually abused? Did the first person you fell in love with betray you in the most painful way?

Laura was utterly destroyed by her father's abandonment of her family and his continual rejection of her during her formative years. She had a chronic fear of being abandoned. When she started dating Troy, she did everything she could to keep him from leaving her. Her logical mind said he was abusive and unfaithful. But her emotional baggage refused to be abandoned. It was only when she recognized this and was healed from these wounds that she was able to kick Troy to the curb and move on.

We do not realize how our emotional baggage dictates the dating choices we make. But it's of paramount importance that we deal with this baggage before we make a marriage decision that we will regret for the rest of our lives. This is not a book on emotional healing so I can't go into this topic in sufficient detail to guide you in your journey toward healing. I can tell you this though, if there ever was a girl with daddy issues it was me. These issues affected my dating choices, friendships, and self-esteem for many years. I will always be grateful to God that by the time Denver came along, I was over those daddy issues and my choice to marry him was based on a clear logical decision enhanced by being madly in love rather than dictated by emotional baggage.

Don't feel however that you have to be totally healed in order to get into the right relationship. The right person can be an invaluable partner and confidante on your healing journey. Denver was a big help in making me more trusting. His solid morals and complete devotion to me made me realize that not all men were like my father. I never thought I could feel so secure in a relationship.

I encourage you to go to God with your emotional baggage. Ask him to show you the full contents of that suitcase and to take you on a healing journey. Submit to His leading. Meditate on the relevant scriptures until they become a part of who you are. Consider counseling. Read books that relate to your specific emotional baggage. Cry it out. Wipe your tears. Then cry some more. Emotional healing has layers like an onion. Let God be the guide on your journey.

Work on your appearance

You can work on your appearance if you need to. Oh how could I say something so unspiritual? I recently tried to match up two of my friends. The guy took one look at the girl's photo and said *"no thanks."* Personally I think she is a beautiful person, but the guy refused to even get to know her based on her looks. We may argue that he is shallow, and maybe he is. Or maybe he is just realistic and knows what he is attracted to.

The fact is that people are not attracted to flaky skin and chapped heels. Now you don't have to necessarily be a beauty queen or as absolutely mind-blowingly gorgeous as I am (if you just looked at my picture at the back and said *"huh?"*, then you need to get your eyes checked☺). But you should do what you can to make yourself physically attractive. This goes equally for men as for women. Men are first attracted by sight, and then they look deeper. I wish I could tell you otherwise, but that's just reality. Women are also not attracted to men who look unhealthy or unkempt.

Work on your wardrobe

Someone once told me that Christian women should dress in such a way as to hide the curves on their body. That person is wrong. The Bible does teach women to dress modestly, but modesty does not mean going Amish.

> *Do not let your adornment be merely outward – arranging the hair, wearing gold, or putting on fine apparel – rather let it be the hidden person of the heart … (1 Peter 3:3-4)*

Notice that this verse does not say you should NOT do your hair and wear make-up. It says do not let that be the depth of your beauty. In addition to being an inwardly beautiful person, dress in a way that makes you as attractive as possible without compromising modesty. This book isn't about giving you rules to follow, so pray about it and use your discretion.

Cleanse your relationships

Show me your friends and I'll show you who you are. Get rid of that guy whom you call as a boyfriend substitute when you are lonely but have no intention of dating. Say goodbye to the bestie who hates men and will be toxic to any relationship you try to develop. I don't have to list them all. There are more crazy people and dysfunctional relationships than I can find paper to list. But you know who they are. They are the people you cannot take into your marriage. A good yardstick is to ask yourself *"How would I feel if my spouse had a relationship like this?"* If the answer is negative, then wish them well and lovingly tell them to hit the road. Remember, Abraham had to separate from Lot before God fully blessed him.

Good healthy relationships filled with love are the perfect cure for the pain and loneliness that often rears its ugly head in the lives of singles from time to time.

Do we need to break soul ties with exes?

The term *"soul tie"* was made popular in a book by Gary Greenwald called *"Seductions Exposed."* It is typically defined as an emotional bond or connection that unites you with someone else. Although the Bible does not use the term soul tie, it does say,

> ... *do you not know that he who is joined to a harlot is one body with her? For "the two," He says, "shall become one flesh." But he who is joined to the Lord is one spirit with Him* ... *(1 Corinthians 6:16-17)*

The expression *"shall become one flesh"* is exactly the same expression used of the marriage relationship. This means that sex with a harlot has the same effect as being married to someone. Many people will testify that if they have an affair, they find it hard to get that person out of their mind. Do you find yourself thinking about an ex over and over again? Even someone with whom you had an awful relationship?

The problem with soul ties is that it is not a Biblical terminology. But based on how it is defined and described, I am convinced that what people call soul ties are really strongholds. That is a Bible term. In our first book, *"small devil, BIG GOD"*, we talked about strongholds and how to use the Word of God to pull them down.

There are many reasons you could find yourself thinking or fantasizing about an ex. It could be that you are still in love with them or have feelings for them. If this is someone you cannot be married to for whatever reason, then ask God to take those feelings away from you.

It is also possible that there is a small aspect of that relationship that you long for. You may have absolutely no desire for a relationship with that person, but there is one small aspect of the relationship that you can't get out of your mind. Just confess this to God. It may or may not be a sin. But we can go to God with our weaknesses and faults and confess them to Him. Pulling down strongholds essentially means to change your pattern of thinking with regards to this person.

When Jesus was confronted with temptations, He used the Word of God – it is written. Strongholds are patterns of wrong thinking that are deeply ingrained in our subconscious. We battle against strongholds by using the truth of God's Word. In the classic spiritual warfare chapter (Ephesians 6), we are commanded to have our loins gird about with truth and to wield the sword of the Spirit, which is the Word of God. Replace the wrong thinking with what God's Word says.

If you have close Christian friends you can confide in, then confess your faults to them as well. Let them pray for and with you as you help each other through.

Forgive

> *For if you forgive men their trespasses, your heavenly Father will also forgive you. But if you do not forgive men their trespasses, neither will your Father forgive your trespasses. … (Matthew 6:14-15)*

If you have issues with others (parents, exes, men in general), you need to forgive and get rid of bitterness from your life. Resentment makes you unattractive. I have heard some single Christians speak, and the bitterness that they exude is evident to anyone who hears them. Any potential mate will sense this immediately and keep their distance. This could be one reason why the right guy or the right girl seems totally unattracted to you. Search yourself and take any resentment to God in prayer.

Examine yourself

Do you find that you keep attracting only one kind of guy or girl – losers and users? There must be a reason for this. Take a close look at yourself. There must be something about you that is attracting the wrong type of person and repelling the right type of person. Ask yourself why you keep choosing the same kind of person and making the same mistake over and over again. Take an honest look at your flaws and ask God to search you and to cleanse you.

Check also to see if there are other things in you that turn off potential mates. Are you still *"hung up"* on your ex? Are you a feminist because the world says you are supposed to be? Do you believe women should be chained to a stove? You are entitled to believe whatever you wish, but these things have social consequences.

Would you date you?

Look at yourself and realistically think about qualities you may have that would turn off potential suitors and put a strain on any marriage you get into. Are you are shopaholic who is in debt? Are you an alcoholic? A hoarder? A chronic workaholic? Does your apartment look like ground-zero? What qualities do you have that you would not want in a spouse? You are not changing who you are intrinsically in order to attract someone. You are improving yourself and dealing with flaws so you can embrace the future you dream of. Don't try to change all on your own. Allow God to change you, but you must want to change.

Get a mentor

> *... the older women likewise, that they be reverent in behavior, not slanderers, not given to much wine, teachers of good things – that they admonish the young women to love their husbands, to love their children, to be discreet, chaste, homemakers, good, obedient to their own husbands, that the word of God may not be blasphemed.*
>
> *Likewise, exhort the young men to be sober-minded*
>
> *... Titus 2:2-6*

These verses teach us that older men and women should serve in a mentoring role for younger Christian men and women. If your church does not have a formal mentorship program, you can do this informally. Find a married couple that you respect and ask them to mentor you. Get them involved in the process of helping you to find a husband or wife and vetting them.

When Denver and I were courting, I took him to my pastor, my spiritual mother, my mentors, my family and my trusted friends. He passed with flying colors, they all loved him. When we look at someone through glasses colored by love, desperation to get married and just a wee bit of lust, they tend to look amazing. Fatal flaws are often blotted out and look like endearing idiosyncrasies. It is best to let those persons in your life, whom you trust, guide you in this important decision. If they are all raising red flags, you need to slam the brakes and take another look.

Pray

Most of all, pray. When I realized that I was taking too long to find a husband, a Christian friend and I decided that we needed to take time-off from our jobs and to pray and fast for a month. We survived on one meal a day for one month. We had various pastors pray for and with us. During this time, we prayed for God to cleanse us of anything that was not pleasing to Him. We cried, we confessed our sins, we re-consecrated our lives, we surrendered all, and we relinquished control to God. My friend took a little longer to find her husband, but for me the result was almost immediate. Within 2 months of ending that prayer-and-fast, Denver and I were matched on eHarmony.

For whatever reason, this is the trial that you face in life. It may not be the one you would like to face. But count it all joy. Learn the lesson that God is teaching you through this trial. Learn it quickly. Don't keep yourself in this trial longer than is necessary by throwing spiritual tantrums and being upset with God or losing focus on the finish line. The quicker you get through this trial the quicker you reach the wedding dress (or tuxedo) at the end of this dark tunnel.

Give thanks with a grateful heart. Give thanks even when it hurts. Focus on your other blessings. Don't murmur like the children of Israel. I am sure you have a lot to be thankful for. Close your eyes for one minute and picture life without two functioning eyes. Then open them and give thanks.

In the presence of God, all pain and hurt will dissolve. Just spend that time in prayer and let the healing begin.

MYTH #5

OVER-COMPLICATING IT

In this chapter

We will learn the various ways in which Christians tend to make life more complicated that God intended. There are things we do that unnecessarily narrow our pool of eligible partners and make it harder for us to get married.

Chapter outline

- Dive stupid
- A Biblical perspective on marriage
- Looking for perfection
- Trying to achieve perfection first
- Trying to eradicate lust
- Ignoring the *"friend-zone"*
- Trying to find contentment in your singleness
- Fear of marriage
- Waiting till you are the right age to marry
- How the devil has shaped modern society
- Courting for too long
- Don't take long to be wrong
- God's design is simple

Dive stupid

Laura Wilkinson is a former United States platform diver who won a gold medal at the Summer Olympics of 2000. This was the first gold medal for a female American platform diver since 1964. She also competed at the 2004 and 2008 Olympics. In a television interview, she outlined her master strategy for executing the perfect dive.

"I dive stupid"

So, there you have it. The key to executing the perfect dive is to *"dive stupid."* What on earth did she mean by that?

After countless hours of training, a diver's body learns a routine. It knows exactly how to negotiate gravity, when to flip, when to twist and when to straighten out so it could execute the correct number of rotations and land in the water at the right angle. The body knows what to do. An athlete begins to run into problems when they start overthinking things. A dive takes place in a fraction of a second. A diver cannot mentally navigate a dive while in midair. They are supposed to do it by muscle memory. Once they start overthinking it, then they start doing things wrong. They overcomplicate it. Then they must go back to the drawing board and retrain their body while deactivating their brain. They must *"dive stupid."*

This is so true of Christians looking for a husband or wife. God designed the process to be simple and straightforward. But we have overcomplicated it and made it more difficult than it should be. People in the Bible found their husbands and wives without much effort. They just took a wife. It was a natural easy process. But today with all our modern misconceptions about waiting for God's perfect will in God's perfect timing, finding a mate has become one of the most arduous decisions facing the single Christian.

A Biblical perspective on marriage

Marriage is an important decision. But it is possible to make it more complicated than it really is. It is also possible to underplay its importance. You definitely don't want to marry the wrong person, as this may be detrimental. At the same time, you don't want to take forever to get married while your entire youth passes you by. God designed it so that people would marry young. Therefore the process cannot be as hard as we sometimes make it out to be. We must have a Biblical perspective on marriage. Make sure you choose wisely. But at the same time, don't overcomplicate it. Take your time without procrastinating.

Let's add some perspective. Marriage is not eternal. 1 Corinthians 13:13 says there are three things – faith, hope and love. Love is the greatest of the three because love is eternal while the other two are only for this life. Well, marriage is only for this life as well. Jesus clearly taught that we will not be married in the afterlife.

> *For in the resurrection they neither marry nor are given in marriage, but are like angels of God in heaven ... (Matthew 22:30)*

In the movie *"Gladiator"*, there is a scene at the end when Russell Crowe's character dies and is reunited with his wife and son in the afterlife. The movie ends with them running through the meadows in slow motion – together forever. It's a really great movie. But that's not how the afterlife is going to be. Jesus made it crystal clear that when you are married, that ends when this life is over. Marriage is temporal. If you wish to run through the meadows in slow motion, do it now because you won't be doing it when you get to heaven.

~~~~~~
God's design was that single Christians meet early in life, marry and procreate. It is that simple.
~~~~~~

Paul takes this idea even further. Because time is short, he is advocating that everyone remains in the same state they're in if they could help it.

> *I suppose therefore that this is good because of the present distress – that it is good for a man to remain as he is ... But this I say, brethren, the time is short, so that from now on even those who have wives should be as though they had none ... (1 Corinthians 7:26,29)*

Married people, life is short, don't get divorced and have to start all over again. Single people, life is short, don't jump into marriage and upend your entire life. Of course, he makes it clear that this is not a rule. Single people could get married. But he thinks remaining single is better. Paul clearly did not think that getting married is as big a deal as we often make it out to be. We must put it in proper perspective.

Now, I need to make this point abundantly clear. I am NOT saying that marriage isn't important. Of course it is. I am simply trying to find the right balance. Again let me reiterate: make sure you take time to choose wisely, but don't overcomplicate it. Here are some of the ways in which people tend to overcomplicate things, and as a result end up remaining single longer than they should.

Looking for perfection

When I was looking for a wife, I remember distinctly that I did not want a perfect woman. I wanted to find Ms. Right, but I didn't want her first name to be Always. I actually dated someone like that – who thought she was little miss perfect. That was the absolute worst relationship ever. That relationship lasted an epic 4 weeks. And for 2 of those 4 weeks, she was angry with me. I can't even remember now why she was angry. But thank God He gave me a glimpse into what being married to her would be like.

You don't want to date a perfect person. They are never wrong. They will never ever admit they are wrong. And honestly, I found it so much more endearing when a woman had human flaws and was down-to-earth.

Leona was also little miss perfect. She was a serial dater. She would fall madly in love, and then after about 6 months she would move on as soon as the guy showed any characteristic that did not meet her high expectations. She was beautiful and had no problems finding replacements. She reached her mid-50s before finally getting married. That marriage only lasted 4 years. She longs for the stability of marriage but does not know how to accept flaws in her partner and how to grow together.

If you are looking for perfection, you will never find it in a human person. The best relationships are the ones where people grow together. Two imperfect people get married with all their flaws and shortcomings, and they vow to stay together and to love each other for life.

I once heard a sermon by an old pastor who was married for over 50 years. He said that he and his wife decided early on that divorce was never going to be an option. They banished that word from their vocabulary. Whatever they went through, however mad they were at each other, they both determined that they would resolve it without playing the divorce card. 50 plus years later, he could attest that they never once considered divorce. Murder maybe, but never divorce. The key to never getting divorced is … never getting divorced.

The happiest couples I know are those who grew together. It was not two perfect people who got married, but rather two very imperfect people who grew together to the point where you could barely tell them apart. That's what I want. Indira and I have been married for just over 7 years. We can't claim 50 years of marriage. We don't claim to know it all. But we have grown a lot together.

People say that I am a lot happier now than before. I smile more. Also they didn't really like me before, but they like me now. Indira has also learned to be a lot more trusting and secure. We have both grown, and by the grace of God, we pray that we will continue to grow together for another 43 years and more. 7 years may not be a lot compared to others, but many marriages don't make 7 years. We truly thank God for His grace, and we pray that what we have learned from experience and from scripture will be a blessing to others who are on the same path.

Trying to achieve perfection first

I noted earlier that you should not rush into a relationship until you are ready for marriage. There is a flip side of this coin. You can wait too long to be ready for marriage. This typically happens when people are trying to get everything else in life sorted out first – their education, their career, their home – so that when they get married, it would be smooth sailing. Marriage will actually be a lot better if you have to endure some rough times together so you can build a life together and grow together.

One of the things that delayed me from getting married was the emphasis on my career. I needed to get my Masters degree first. I needed to get my PhD first. I needed to get a stable job first. All of these things were very noble pursuits. The problem is that the years kept ticking by. Many other people get married early in life, and they figure out their career paths afterward. This way they get the opportunity to grow together. If I could do it all over again, I would have preferred that any day. My biggest regret is that Indira and I did not meet earlier in life.

Many of us are too indecisive. Sometimes we want everything to be perfect before we get married. The problem with this approach is that when you finally do get married, your husband or wife will feel like an intruder in the life that you have successfully built independently of them. Leave room for both of you to grow together.

I know someone who was planning to get married in 2017. She spent years planning that wedding. Then she postponed it to 2018. Why? Because two of her cousins were already getting married in 2017. There are so many things that could delay you getting married. Why would you unnecessarily add to that list?

Trying to eradicate lust

I even know of people who refuse to declare themselves ready for marriage until they overcome *"lust."* I find this to be the most laughable thing I have ever heard. And these people did not come up with that on their own. There are preachers and authors telling them that if they have a lust problem before they get married, then they will just take their lust problem into the marriage. If that were true, then why did Paul say *"if they cannot exercise self-control, let them marry"* (1 Corinthians 7:9)? Why didn't he tell them to get rid of the lust problem first?

I believe these people fail to understand the difference between lust and sex addiction. If you are a sex addict, then you need to sort that out before you get married. But many people (especially men) have been labeled as having a *"lust problem"* when in fact they are perfectly normal. If you have a sex addiction, then you need professional help. But sexual thoughts and sex addiction are two entirely separate things.

Lust is similar to sex in that it magically ceases to be a sin within the context of marriage. Sex in itself is not a sin, only if done outside of marriage. The same thing is true of lust. Lust in itself is not a bad thing. Lust for someone you are not married to is a sin just as bad as adultery. But lust for someone you are married to is not a sin.

Typically people associate lust with erotic thoughts. But here is a revelation for you: lust does not mean thought. It means desire. Lust is a strong desire with an element of intent. The Greek word *"epithumeó"* is translated lust (Matthew 5:28), covet (Romans 7:7), and desire (1 Timothy 3:1). Notably, in 1 Timothy 3:1, we see that lust can be a positive thing sometimes. It just needs to be properly directed and properly handled. In Matthew 9:3-4, on the other hand, Jesus used the word *"enthymēseis"* to describe reflections or thoughts. So we see two different Greek words being used in scripture to refer to lust and thoughts. They are not the same.

I am not trying to downplay the seriousness of lust, but merely thinking sexual thoughts is not the same thing as lust. Lust is when you have an uncontrollable desire for sex, when you covet someone sexually, and when your heart is set upon them. Of course if this person is your husband or wife, then it is not a sin. That's the amazing thing. So based on this, the solution to a *"lust problem"* is actually getting married. That is exactly what Paul told the Corinthians.

I am also convinced from Scripture that lust is a sin of intention rather than a sin of thought. If you read 2 Samuel 13, you will see what lust really is. Amnon had a burning desire for his half-sister Tamar, so much so that he felt sick. Read how he plotted and schemed to seduce her. That is what lust is – the thing that drove Amnon to do what he did. Once you realize this, you will see that Christian teenagers don't have a lust problem, they simply have a hormonal issue.

The reason sexual thoughts flood people's minds, especially when they are in a romantic relationship, is because of a hormone called testosterone. It's hormonal. It's not demonic or carnal. Testosterone is at a record high during our adolescent years. Also in the early stages of a romantic relationship, there is a testosterone spike in both the male and the female, and that is why it is very difficult to keep your hands off each other. Testosterone is not a sin. That is how God designed the human body. God designed it that way so that people would get married quickly and have children. The solution to this *"problem"* is marriage. This is also the reason why getting into a relationship when you are not ready for marriage is a bad idea. You won't be able to control the passions.

How do you know if you have a lust problem? Simple. You don't have a lust problem if you find yourself thinking sexual thoughts about the opposite sex. That only means you are heterosexual and healthy. You have a lust problem when you find yourself scheming and planning how you can *"bed"* as many partners as you could. *"What is the best way to seduce this person? Pretend to be interested in marriage, then gradually push the boundaries."* When you start thinking like that, you have crossed over from thoughts (*enthymēseis*) into lust (*epithumeó*). This is what Jesus was talking about in Matthew 5:28. You have already committed adultery.

So don't allow hormones and an active imagination to prevent you from getting married. That was designed to encourage you to marry. Unless you have some kind of sex addiction, porn addiction or an evil heart of lust, you don't have a lust problem that marriage won't cure. Don't put undue condemnation on yourself and others, and don't allow others to put condemnation on you.

Ignoring the *"friend-zone"*

The *"friend-zone"* is not a Biblical concept. The friend-zone refers to the difficulty some people have in transitioning from a platonic friendship into a romantic relationship. So because of this, they say that they fell into the friendship-zone and they can't come out.

The statistics show that 40% of married couples were platonic friends before they got married. So this is very much a personal matter. If you feel that there is an eligible member of the opposite sex that you consider a brother or sister, but you cannot for the life of you think of them in romantic terms, then look for someone else. But there is no rule that says you can't turn a friendship into a relationship.

Trying to find contentment in your singleness

Has anyone ever told you that in order to prepare for marriage, you must first find contentment in your singleness? They tell single Christians that they must learn to *"savor their singleness"* otherwise they are not ready for marriage. I promise you I am not making this up.

Now, there are numerous scriptures that teach us to be content. Usually they mean to be content with the blessings God has given us, and not be greedy for material things (for example, Luke 3:14; Philippians 4:11; 1 Timothy 6:6,8; Hebrews 13:5). There is no scripture that says to be content in your singleness.

Telling people that they need to be content in their singleness before they can get married is like saying you need to find contentment in being unemployed before you can find a job. Check out what Paul said to single Christians.

> *For I wish that all men were even as I myself. But each one has his own gift from God ... (1 Corinthians 7:7)*

Let's read between the lines to see what wisdom is buried in this verse. Paul wished that everyone could remain single like he was, but acknowledged that they couldn't because they didn't have that gift. It stands to reason that Paul had a gift that enabled him to remain single without yearning for marriage. You may call this the gift of celibacy.

How do you know if you have the gift of celibacy? You would have no desire to get married, no yearning, no burning passion. You would be content to be single just like Paul was. Even the Apostle Paul acknowledged that this was a gift that not everyone has.

Therefore, a single person who does not have the gift of celibacy cannot be totally content being single. It is just not how God designed us. This is yet another myth that single Christians are being bombarded with.

Fear of marriage

Sam had an abusive mother – physically and emotionally. When Sam grew up, he had a chronic fear of getting into a relationship. He did not realize how many of his actions were dictated by this fear. He would immediately find a deal-breaker with any potential love interest. He once wrote off a girl simply because her car was disorganized. Even if things seemed to be going well with someone he was dating, he would find a way to sabotage it. Eventually Sam started to see a counsellor who helped him to recognize and confront this fear. Soon he was able to enter into a relationship with a very understanding lady who helped him along his journey. Today they are happily married and have adopted two beautiful children.

Many others are afraid to make that transition from single life to married life. The longer you remain single, the harder that transition becomes because you become more and more entrenched in your singleness.

When I first met Denver and started to get to know him, I thought he was too good to be true. I kept waiting for the other shoe to drop. I observed him carefully to see if he was secretly gay. I subtly checked to ascertain whether he was a wife beater. I believed that he had some secret psychosis, and if I looked deeply enough I would find it. After 8 years of knowing him, being married to him for over 7, I can safely say he has no deep-seated psychosis … other than a corny sense of humor.☺

This is an example of how fear can play with our minds. Fear can make us act irrationally and even sabotage a perfectly good relationship. Fear is exacerbated especially if you have had bad experiences or if you have seen those around you suffer. We need to deal with fear.

Now I am not saying that we should just cast aside reasonable caution and jump into a relationship with someone who, for example, shows all the signs of being a serial killer, but don't let fear keep you from what may be the relationship you have been longing for.

Waiting till you are the right age to marry

Today the average age at which people get married in North America is 28. In 1990, the average was 24 years old. What is the best age to marry? Of course, the answer depends on so many things, not the least of which is your maturity and readiness for marriage.

In the Bible days, people generally got married younger than today. Back then, life was indeed much simpler than it is now. The major reason people are taking longer and longer to get married is because they perceive that the risk of divorce is too high. They worked really hard to build a life for themselves. The last thing they need is a bad marriage to ruin everything. So they err on the side of caution. Some of them walk away from a relationship when they realize that the other person actually has flaws. Again, this is a question of balance. You don't want to miss major red flags, but at the same time you cannot expect perfection.

How the devil has shaped modern society

In the Bible days, life was simpler. They grew up on a farm, they married someone from their community, and the village raised their kids. There was very little variability in people's lives and careers. People were simple, and they lived simple lives. Their lives were not necessarily easy, but simple. As a result, anybody could have been married to anyone else of the opposite gender, and it would have had a good chance of working.

Times have changed. Today, our lives are complicated. We now have myriads of personality types that are often incompatible with others. We have different love languages. Society has also become much more global. You grow up in one place, then you move to live and work somewhere else a thousand miles away. You probably work for a company that is so big, that you could be transferred to another state or country far away from where you presently live. These things take a deleterious toll on family life and family planning.

Do you believe that these things just happened by chance? We call it progress. We refer to the simplicity of ancient times as *"archaic."* Although God created the earth, He did not create modern society. After God created the earth, He left man in charge to run things, and He chose not to micromanage. The devil has very cleverly orchestrated the evolution of modern society to what it is today – a godless generation.

Once upon a time, men worked while women managed the homes and the children. But some men were abusive, some were adulterous, and their wives could not do anything about it because they were dependents. Young girls observed this and decided that they did not want to be homemakers because they did not want to go through what their mothers went through. Mothers encouraged their daughters to pursue higher learning so they could find good jobs. Today, women have excelled above and beyond men. They can do just about everything men can do and better. They have achieved a high level of independence.

Men have also responded to that change. Today, many men have no interest in getting married because they feel that society has put a lot of pressure on them because of things men did in the past. Have you ever heard the term *"male privilege"*? There is a movement in society that blames Caucasian Christian men for everything that is wrong in the world. Men have responded to this by avoiding the *"marriage trap."* Some men are more interested in having temporary sex partners than a wife. The reason is fear of marriage.

Now women have responded to that development by becoming even less dependent on men, to the extent that many women are losing their interest in marriage altogether. They have decided that they can be *"players"* as well.

This is how modern society has evolved. With each passing generation, the devil has more deeply perpetuated the belief that the Biblical family ideal is not tenable – that our lives are way too complicated for the Biblical idea of family. I am not saying that we can change it or reverse it. But it is important to be aware of these things and to distinguish between God's design and what we actually see around us.

<u>God's design was that single Christians meet early in life, marry and procreate. It is that simple.</u> God's design was never for our careers to be more important than our families. He also never intended for family to place such a high amount of pressure on people. It was supposed to be simple. God designed it to be simple. We are the ones who have overcomplicated things.

Having said all of that, I am perfectly aware that society was not perfect in Biblical times. Women had no rights and were treated as property. But in the midst of those imperfections in society, Paul urged men to love their wives as Christ loved the church and gave Himself for it.

Now, in the midst of different societal problems, Christians need to be mindful of Biblical principles, without which we get sucked into the world order and become no different from non-Christians. We need to be aware of these things so we can distinguish between God's design and the devil's design.

<u>Courting for too long</u>

You meet someone. You go on a few dates. The butterflies start moving in your stomach. How long should it take you to determine if this person is right for you? How long should you court? The answer to this question depends on a number of things. How old are you? How well do you know yourself? Are you ready for marriage? Generally the younger you are, the longer you should take to get to know the other person. The better you know yourself, the more likely you are to know what you want and whether you have found it, and the less time you will need to court.

In the Bible days, no one dated. Dating is a modern western concept. There was no such thing as long courtships in the Bible. People met, and they got married. Rebekah made her decision to leave her parents' house, and she married Isaac the same day she met him. It was simple.

Of course, as we noted earlier, they could do this because their lives were a lot simpler than ours. We don't have that luxury. But even though our society is different, there are principles in scripture that remain unchanged. We cannot get married within one day of meeting someone, but the Bible favors short courtships over long ones. There are obvious reasons. Paul told the Corinthians:

> ... *to avoid fornication, let every man have his own wife, and let every woman have her own husband ... I say therefore to the unmarried and widows, it is good for them if they abide even as I. But if they cannot contain, let them marry: for it is better to marry than to burn [with passion] ... (1 Corinthians 7:2,8-9, KJV)*

Long courtships make no sense in the light of these scriptures. Courtship is a time where you are going to be hormone-crazy. During the early stages of a romantic relationship, there is a testosterone spike in BOTH the male and female resulting in burning passion. That is a physiological fact. If you intend to wait till after marriage for sex, then a long courtship is going to be r-e-a-l-l-y long. It is unnecessary torture. Unsaved people don't have this problem because they are not waiting for marriage to have sex. But Christians are supposed to be different.

My personal belief is that people should not be in a romantic relationship at all if they are not ready to get married soon. I would not recommend 15-year olds in high school to get into romantic relationships. Studies have shown that people that age cannot even have a mature relationship with their parents. Why rush it? Just have as many friends as you like. Wait until you are close to being ready for marriage before getting into a deep commitment. If you are not ready for marriage, then why are you so interested in being in a relationship? You are doing yourself and your partner a great disservice.

Tori (a member of our Bible Issues Facebook group) was 15 years old when she met Billy (19) at a swim class. A few years later, they found themselves spending more time together – as friends. Although they both considered themselves adults, they acknowledged that they needed to mature a bit before they realized there was the potential of a relationship. While Tori was away studying, Billy came up each weekend to visit, and that's when they knew there was something there. He came up each weekend by choice and they looked forward to seeing each other. They enjoyed each other's company, they spoke on the phone, they learned to laugh together, pray together, and help each other in the final stages of growing up. Tori followed her parents' wishes for her to complete her degree before getting married. She was 25 when they finally got married.

Even though they were young when they met, they were mature enough to realize that they needed to let their friendship develop first before they would be ready for marriage. It took a lot of wisdom for persons that age to acknowledge they were not ready for a relationship, and to wait for the right time. Having said that, once they realized they were ready, it did not take them long to know they had found what they were looking for.

Don't take long to be wrong

Usually when people go on dates, they put on their best behavior. It is generally a good thing to be well-behaved, but that poses a problem. It makes it harder to truly know someone and for them to know the real you. It is only after a few months, that we start letting our guards down and then we discover a new side to the other person. It only takes long because we waste a lot of time trying to impress rather than trying to learn about the other person.

After a few failed relationships, I found myself in my early 30s and still single. I realized that I did not have time to waste playing this silly game of trying to impress women. By this time in my life, I had also gained a lot of self-confidence that I did not have when I was younger. So I started adopting a totally different approach to dating. I knew I wanted someone with a sense of humor. That was a deal-breaker for me. I love to make jokes and look on the lighter side of things. I could not marry someone who was oversensitive and easily offended. So I started testing the other person very early in the dating process. I did not want to take long to be wrong. If I was dating the wrong person, I wanted to find out early.

There was one particular person who called me on the phone non-stop after our first date. But I was not sure she was the one I was looking for. So I decided to put her to the test. Before I tell you what the test was, let me emphatically reassure you that I do NOT believe in polygamy. I believe in monogamous heterosexual marriage OK – my wife being a co-author and all☺. Now that we got that out of the way, here is the test I used.

> ***Me:*** *I believe in the good old days of the Old Testament, when men could have more than one wife. The Old Testament simply said that if the man could afford it, he could have more wives as long as he provides separate living arrangements for them. Yeah, the good old days.*
>
> ***Her:*** *Well could a woman have more than one husband?*
>
> ***Me:*** *NOPE. The Bible only allows men to have multiple wives, not the other way around. You are being completely unscriptural.*
>
> ***Her:*** *Well what about your dad, did he have two wives?*

Me: *Umm, no. My dad was a school teacher all his life, he could only afford one wife. Duh!*

The non-stop phone calls stopped after that. She later told me *"I cannot be with someone who believes in polygamy."* When I explained to her that I was joking, she said, *"You do not joke about something like that."*

Do I believe in polygamy? Of course not! I wanted to see how she would react. I wanted to see if she had a sense of humor. So as far as I was concerned, I did not lose true love. I simply made the whole process a lot shorter, so I could move on. I am pretty sure if I had said that to Indira while we were courting, she would have told me *"Before you take a second wife, I think you should meet my mom. Then you'll decide whether you can handle two mothers-in-law."* That's what I was looking for.

I understand that not everyone would be comfortable with those kinds of tests and tactics. But it sure helped me to eradicate first date jitters. Maybe you prefer what Kate Jovin did. She is a former Jeopardy champion who always had her first date in the cemetery. Yip. In her home town, there is a cemetery that contains a picturesque garden, which is perfect for picnicking. She said that suggesting the cemetery for a first date helps her to filter out any guy who does not like weird women.

God's design is simple

Don't take long to be wrong. Life is too short. There are so many ways in which we overcomplicate things, when God designed it to be simple. You need to be able to determine very quickly if you have found what you are looking for, or if you need to keep searching. My personal belief is that when you are mature enough to be ready for marriage, and when you know yourself well enough and exactly what you are looking for, it should not take you longer than 3 months to know for sure if someone is right for you or not.

MYTH #6

BEING TOO FUSSY

In this chapter

We will investigate what compatibility means. Does compatibility mean we must have the same ministry? Does it mean we have the same interests? The same denomination? What does the Bible teach about compatibility? What does the Bible actually teach that we should be looking for?

Chapter outline

- Is ministry a requirement to get married?
- Married people have divided interests
- Is ministry compatibility a thing?
- The key to a happy marriage
- Don't narrow your playing field
- Differences are OK
- Should Christians marry outside of their denomination?
- Personal preferences
- What should you be looking for?

Is ministry a requirement to get married?

A few years ago, the head pastor of a church was counseling a couple who was planning to get married. One of the elders of the church was also present. At a certain point in the counseling session, the elder interrupted and stated his objection to the marriage on the grounds that *"they have different ministries."* The elder believed that because the man and the woman had different callings on their lives, they should not be married – even though they were both Christians. They were not *"ministry compatible."* The pastor looked at him with exasperation and said, *"People don't get married for ministry."*

Christians are commonly taught that God will bring their husband and wife to them in His timing. But in order to *"receive"* that person, you must be in the middle of God's will occupying yourself with the work of the Lord. In fact, I used to teach this when I was younger. I used to draw two squiggly lines on the board that represented God's perfect will for two Christians – and the place where the two lines merged into one – that is called God's perfect timing. I used to teach this, I am embarrassed to say. But later on I realized the error of my ways and I abandoned these unscriptural teachings.

The Bible does teach us to occupy ourselves with the work of the Lord (Luke 19:13). But that has absolutely nothing to do with finding a husband or wife. There is absolutely nothing in scripture that says a husband or wife is a reward for faithful service to God. No siree. There is also no one in the Bible who found their husband or wife that way.

"Well didn't God bring Eve to Adam while he was busy tending the garden?" you ask in a whiny nasal voice.☺

> *And the Lord God said, "It is not good that man should be alone; I will make him a helper comparable to him."* ... Genesis 2:18

We have already seen that Adam and Eve had a situation that is different from everyone else who ever lived. But yes God did create Eve as a *"help meet"* for Adam – meaning a *"helper suitable"* for him. Did this mean Eve was created to be a ministry partner? If you say *"yes"*, then I should ask you, what exactly was Adam's ministry? Tending the garden? Naming the animals? Did he really need a helper for that?

God created Eve because he recognized that Adam was alone. He created her not because Adam needed a ministry helper, but because Adam needed 1) companionship and 2) a woman to procreate.

Married people have divided interests

The Bible actually teaches that single people are more effective in ministry than married people because they have more time to focus on ministry.

> *He who is unmarried cares for the things of the Lord – how he may please the Lord. But he who is married cares about the things of the world – how he may please his wife … The unmarried woman cares about the things of the Lord, that she may be holy both in body and in spirit. But she who is married cares about the things of the world – how she may please her husband … (1 Corinthians 7:32-34)*

So if it's all about ministry, it would be better to not get married. If God wanted to keep you focused on ministry, then He would not send you a husband or wife. He would keep you single.

Having said that, Indira and I are very much involved in ministry together. We are a team. But God did not help us to find each other while we were busy occupying ourselves with the work of the Lord. We were both active in ministry WHEN we met, but this was not HOW we met. We met online on an internet dating site. And we are very much involved in ministry together now, but our meeting and marriage had nothing to do with ministry.

In fact, I will show you in this chapter that any two (genuine) Christians can have ministry compatibility if they so desire. Ministry compatibility is not something you need to worry about since it is not a requirement for marriage. It happens automatically. Once you both are genuine Christians, there is no way your ministries could be incompatible. It is impossible.

Is ministry compatibility a thing?

We know two Christians who both felt a call of God upon their lives to be missionaries. In university, they were part of the same Christian group, they became good friends and fell in love with each other. However, they decided not to pursue a relationship because, although they were both called to be missionaries, they felt God was calling them into different geographic locations. What do you think about that? Are they really committed to God or are they really crazy?

Your answer to this question may depend on how involved you are in Christian work. I know that different Christians have different levels of involvement in ministry. But the issue here is not really how involved you are, but rather what place you attribute to ministry in your Christian walk. Is it all about ministry? Or is ministry something you do in addition to everything else? Is ministry more important than your family, or vice versa?

For some Christians, there is a heavy emphasis on getting married to someone with a compatible ministry. If you marry someone with a different calling, then you could ruin your own call and not fulfill your purpose – so the teaching goes. <u>That is a myth</u>. That is a myth that unnecessarily narrows your pool of eligible marriage partners and significantly reduces your chances of finding someone to marry. Look at the following scripture:

> *There are <u>diversities of gifts</u>, but the <u>same Spirit</u>. There are <u>differences of ministries</u>, but the <u>same Lord</u>. And there are <u>diversities of activities</u>, but it is the <u>same God</u> who works all in all … (1 Corinthians 12:4-6)*

These verses tell us in very plain speech that although people in the church have different gifts, different ministries and different activities, it is one God, one Spirit, one Lord. The Bible also likens the church to the human body. The different members have different functions, but they are all interconnected by a single central nervous system. We all need each other. We cannot function without each other. The hand cannot say to the eye *"I don't need you."* No part of the body is independent. All the parts are different, yet all the parts complement one another perfectly.

That's also how the church is. We have different ministries – preaching, teaching, helps, giving, administration, etc. There are pastors, Sunday School teachers, missionaries. In the church, God has also called business men, school teachers, police officers, etc. They all have a part to play in the body of Christ. You may think that a police officer's job is not a Christian ministry, but look at the instructions Paul gave to secular workers.

> *… whatever you do, do it heartily, as to the Lord and not to men, knowing that from the Lord you will receive the reward of the inheritance; for you serve the Lord Christ … (Colossians 3:23-24)*

We have a reward in heaven for whatever secular work we do. Even though it is not a spiritual type of ministry or church work, it is still the Lord's work. We are all connected by one Holy Spirit. Remember God's will is not so much what you do but how you do it.

So after all of that, if there are two genuine Christians – who are both saved by the same blood of Jesus, who have the same Holy Spirit living in them, who are both called according to God's purposes – how could their ministries not be compatible? They may not seem compatible to you, but they are perfectly compatible to God.

In other words, there is no rule that says if you are a lawyer, you must also be married to another professional. There is no rule that says if you are a pastor, you must be married to someone with a teaching ministry. There are successful pastors who are married to homemakers, school teachers, fellow ministers, and professionals. A missionary can marry an engineer or another missionary. Anyone can marry anyone as long as they are both Christians and they are of opposite genders. Compatibility does not have to be forced. It is automatic.

Donna was a worship leader in her church. When she got engaged to Newman, her friends were concerned. Although Newman was a Christian, he did not have a spiritual ministry. He worked in a store, and was not very active in church. Donna's friends said he was not anointed, he was not spiritual. Some of them even questioned his salvation. She asked me for my advice. I asked her, *"Do you have any doubts that he is a genuine Christian?"* She had no doubt. Then I asked her, *"Was he born a man?"* Again yes. *"Then forget what people are saying. Life is too short and you are not getting younger."*

They have now been married for over 15 years. They love each other. He treats her well. She still leads worship in her church. And over time, Newman discovered that he has a strong call to work with the youths in the church. Donna's friends may not be impressed with the spiritual level of his ministry. But God knows his heart and will reward him for the work he does. I would say I gave her good counsel.

The key to a happy marriage

Very often, single people are taught that the key to a happy marriage is finding someone who is compatible with you. Compatibility is great. But it's not the key to marital bliss. The key to a happy marriage is two genuine Christians living godly lives and following Biblical principles. It is when you genuinely love your spouse more than yourself. This is not just a quality for married people, but for all Christians.

> *Let nothing be done through selfish ambition or conceit, but in lowliness of mind let each esteem others better than himself ... Philippians 2:3*

The key to a happy marriage is the same as the key to a fulfilling Christian life.

A few years ago, Indira and I were blessed to be able to travel to Peru. On our way to Machu Picchu, we stayed in a city called Cuzco which is located 11,000 feet above sea level. We had concerns about the oxygen level at that altitude and something called altitude sickness because Indira is asthmatic.

On our first night there, I started vomiting and feeling sick. Neither of us was expecting me to feel sick. We were terrified because we had no idea what to do. Would I die from oxygen deprivation? Did we need to get a helicopter to airlift us back to Lima? How would we even begin to make something like that happen? We called in a doctor who tested my blood oxygen level, and it was good. It turned out to be motion sickness from the drive to the hotel. Sigh of relief. He gave me two Dramamine tablets, which I promptly vomited out. Then he decided to give me a Dramamine injection instead. Less nausea, more drowsiness – I could live with that.

Later that night, when the drowsiness from the injection was setting in, Indira started vomiting uncontrollably. Now we were worried. She was the one with asthma. Here was I with my still sick and drowsy self, trying to be there for my wife. We called back the doctor, who tested her oxygen level, and it was good. It turned out to be food poisoning from her lunch. Another shot of Dramamine.

That experience taught us something very important about our marriage. We were both sick yet more interested in taking care of the other person than our own self. And through that, we came up with a love phrase that we always remind ourselves of when we have to face testing times.

Me taking care of you

You taking care of me

And God taking care of us

There are many ways in which we are compatible. But there are other ways in which we are not. It is not compatibility that makes our marriage happy, but putting the other person first. All the single years of continually surrendering all to God served to teach us how to put ourselves last and to put the other person first. We truly thank God now for those experiences.

Don't narrow your playing field

Because many Christians are trying to force compatibility based on their own understanding and their own perception of things, they have greatly narrowed their field and they have eliminated a lot of people who could have been very good husbands or wives for them. This misunderstanding of spirituality is making it harder for them to get married. This is what the Bible calls *"leaning on your own understanding."*

If you buy a Hawaiian pizza, you will get about 8-12 slices of delicious mouth-watering food. But if you insist on finding a slice with no ham or pineapples, then you are not going to end up with any slices. The more divisions you create, the fewer eligible partners that remain, and the harder it becomes for you to get married. Those divisions only exist in your mind.

When I was younger, I noticed that the single Christians in my church informally divided themselves into two groups – the so-called spiritual ones who cared about spiritual things, and the so-called worldly ones who cared about non-spiritual things. The first group wanted to be pastors, pastor's wives, missionaries, and intercessors. The second group didn't. I also noticed that the church went through a 5 year period where none of those in the so-called spiritual group got married - zero. But people in the other group were getting married. Today a lot of those spiritual ones are still single even though they had desired to get married in *"God's timing."* The reason for this is simple. They unnecessarily narrowed their playing field because of a silly misunderstanding of compatibility, spirituality and ministry.

God has only given one rule to Christians looking to get married – get married to another Christian of the opposite gender. That's it. Anything else is a matter of personal preference. God has made it simple. God has made it in such a way that as long as two genuine Christians marry each other, compatibility is automatic. They will automatically complement each other without even trying.

This myth has caused us to invent compatibility requirements that the Bible does not teach. It has also caused us to be unnecessarily judgmental and divisive. Instead of us embracing the unity of the Holy Spirit, we have now created divisions over ministries and callings. Some people have spiritual ministries, so they should stick together. Some people have business ministries, so they should not intermingle with the spiritual ones. Some have physical helps ministries, and again, they should marry within their kind. The Bible does not impose this requirement on us. We are not divided over our callings, but rather united by the Spirit that called us.

History is replete with great men and women who were married to people who were not considered great, but provided invaluable support. In some cases, they made the other person great. There are so many ways in which two Christians can complement each other, you would be hard pressed to conjure up a scenario where two genuine Christians could be ministry incompatible.

The Bible does not teach that strong Christians should avoid marrying weak Christians. It only teaches that genuine Christians should marry genuine Christians. Whether you are weak or strong depends on so many things. Knowledge is one. Experience is another. We grow through knowledge and through trials and experiences. Sometimes, strong Christians can go through periods where they feel weak. Even Paul felt weak (2 Corinthians 12:9). Also, weak Christians can become strong as they grow in the Lord.

Regarding our two missionary friends that we alluded to earlier, there is no rule that said God called them to be missionaries in a very specific geographic region. God simply called them to be missionaries. They could do missionary work anywhere. We have already seen that God's will for our lives is very flexible. If they had married, they could have served as missionaries together in one location, and God would have still used them mightily. If however, they knew beyond a shadow of a doubt that God had called them to different regions, then they should be obedient to that call.

Differences are OK

When we understand the unity of the Spirit who calls us, we will realize that even if our gifts and callings are different, they are still compatible. As long as we have the same Holy Spirit, even our differences can complement each other.

You don't want to marry a polar opposite but at the same time you don't need someone who is an exact duplicate of you. You need some similarities (especially in spiritual things). But some differences are good as well.

> *Two are better than one, because they have a good reward for their labor. For if they fall, one will lift up his companion. But woe to him who is alone when he falls, For he has no one to help him up … Ecclesiastes 4:9-10*

Two are better than one because when one is weak, the other will be there to strengthen them. Therefore, differences are great, especially if the other person is strong in areas where you are weak, and vice versa. If you are both weak in a certain area, then that provides an opportunity for you to grow together. You don't need to achieve perfection before you marry. Leave room for mutual growth.

Many times we think that we need someone who is very similar to us in order to make a successful marriage. The fact is, being married makes you part of a team of 2 people. On a team, you do not want 2 exact duplicates of each other. You want two persons whose strengths and weaknesses complement each other. This makes the team all the stronger.

Denver is an introvert and I am an outgoing and talkative person. Denver tends to approach new friendships and business associates in a cautious and analytical manner, whereas I tend to be more trusting and open and quite frankly rather naïve at times. Instead of these differences being a source of contention, they have become a way in which we complement each other and we have helped each other to grow. Denver is a lot more outgoing now and I am working on being less naïve.

If you look for someone who is too similar to yourself you narrow the scope of your potential mates. You may also miss out on the enriching experience of growing from being exposed to different perspectives and approaches to life.

Should Christians marry outside of their denomination?

Christ built the church. Man created denominations. At the same time, denominations represent unique beliefs that Christians may have in peripheral issues. None of these peripheral issues have anything to do with salvation, therefore there is nothing in scripture preventing Christians from marrying across denominational lines. However, if you are already married to your denominational beliefs, and you absolutely cannot marry someone who believes differently from you, then you may be best advised to marry within your denomination. That is your preference, but you will be narrowing your playing field. The Bible does not impose this requirement on us. The Bible only requires Christians to marry Christians.

Personal preferences

As I noted earlier, the Bible only gives us one rule when looking for a husband or a wife. Christians should marry other Christians of the opposite gender. Anything additional to that is a matter of personal preference. There is nothing wrong with having personal preferences, but it is important to be mindful of what the scripture says and what your personal requirements are.

For example, if a guy is specifically interested in a woman who is a home maker, that is his choice. He is perfectly entitled to that choice. But the Bible does not impose this requirement. There are actually many churches that believe married women should not work. There are indeed a lot of benefits that could be derived from having a stay-at-home mom. But the Bible does not require this. In fact, the benchmark Proverbs 31 woman is actually a shrewd business woman as well as a home maker. Read it.

Things like height, eye-color, hair-color, skin color, ethnicity, nationality, age differences – these are all peripheral issues that fall under the category of personal preferences. Don't make these things a deal breaker.

I had a list of things I wanted in a wife. But I was wise enough to know that when you meet someone you really love, that list goes out the window. If you meet someone who is a 100% match to what's on your list, that is great. But don't be a slave to a list. Don't throw away a great potential relationship because of something you wrote on a piece of paper. When I made a list of what I wanted in a wife, she was going to be about 2 – 4 years younger than I. Indira is actually 1 year older. Was I going to walk away because of that? That would have made me a colossal idiot, and I would have missed out on the love of a lifetime.

It is great to have your list, and I encourage you to do that. Abraham had a list – although his list only had one item on it. Some people have short lists with a lot of flexibility built into it like I did. Some people have long lists with a lot of specifics like Indira did. Indira had 50 requirements in a husband, and apparently I fit 49 of them – I wasn't good at card games. Other people make their list, but subconsciously when they are making their list, they have a very specific person in mind. Don't be too narrow.

Don't make anything on that list a deal-breaker other than the Biblical requirement that Christians should marry Christians. If you want to be married to a professional Christian man, great. But I should point out that those are not easy to find. There are many professional women who are relaxing that requirement, and actually dating men who earn less than they do. As long as they are both Christians, God is perfectly OK with that. Could you be the head of your home if you make less than your wife? Why not? Headship in the home has nothing to do with who makes more money. The man is the head of the wife just as the Father is the Head of Christ. It is a matter of role and function, not superiority or domination.

Just remember, that as long as you are both Christians, your ministries and callings will automatically complement each other without you trying. Don't make ministry a deal-breaker. Life is too short, and there are way too few eligible Christians around to unnecessarily narrow your playing field.

What should you be looking for?

Instead of looking for ministry compatibility, there are many other desirable godly qualities the Bible actually tells us to look for.

Someone who is not contentious or quarrelsome

> *Better to dwell in a corner of a housetop, than in a house shared with a contentious woman ... (Proverbs 21:9)*

Better to dwell in the wilderness, than with a contentious and angry woman ... (Proverbs 21:19)

It is better to dwell in a corner of a housetop, than in a house shared with a contentious woman ... (Proverbs 25:24)

A continual dripping on a very rainy day And a contentious woman are alike ... (Proverbs 27:15)

Wow! It is better to live on the roof or in the wilderness than with a quarrelsome person.

Proverbs 31 qualities

Proverbs 31 speaks of the virtuous woman, but there is no need to restrict these qualities to women only. Both men and women can strive for the qualities below. These are things to look for in a Christian spouse:

- Trust worthy (vs. 11)
- Hard working (vs. 13)
- Proactive (vs. 14-15) – NOT PASSIVE
- Business savvy (vs. 16)
- Generous to the poor (vs. 20)
- Supportive (vs. 23)
- Wise (vs. 26)
- Kind (vs. 26)
- Caring (vs. 27)
- God-fearing (vs. 30)

Fruit of the Spirit – Galatians 5:22-23

- Love
- Joy
- Peace
- Longsuffering
- Kindness
- Goodness
- Faithfulness
- Gentleness
- Self-control

Other desirable things
- Being true to their word
- They make you stronger
- They are involved in church (if that's what you are looking for)
- They have good relationships with their family
- They have good relationships with other Christians
- They show respect for your family
- They are not easily angered
- They dress appropriately

These things are not necessarily deal breakers. But they are good things to look for. Ultimately, the key is finding a genuine Christian who is genuinely following Christ. Remember if a husband and wife are both genuine Christians and both genuinely following Christ, that is the only compatibility that really matters.

MYTH #7

NOT BEING FUSSY ENOUGH

In this chapter

We will look at the concept of missionary dating. What should we look for and what should we avoid in a potential marriage partner? We will discuss some of the red flags that the Bible talks about, and how to avoid getting trapped in the wrong relationship.

Chapter outline

- 15 lost years
- What is missionary dating?
- Be not unequally yoked
- People do not change
- Being in the wrong relationship for too long
- Being in too many wrong relationships
- Relationship experience counts for nothing
- Dating while you are vulnerable
- How to identify a true Christian
- Avoid certain *"Christians"* as well
- What about people who are divorced?
- Do not ignore red flags
- Be open to God's guidance
- Don't settle

15 lost years

Valerie was divorced because her first husband was unfaithful. During this period of her life, she found Christ, got saved and was on fire for God. Her father was very deep in another religion and he did not appreciate his daughter being a Christian. So he introduced her to a single man looking for a wife. As you would expect, this man was not a Christian. Valerie excitedly told me that she was getting re-married. From the moment she shared the details, I knew this was her father's strategy to draw her back to her old religion. I asked her, *"Is he a born-again Christian?"* She stopped speaking to me after that. She thought she could win him to Christ after she married him.

15 years later, she wrote me and said she was getting divorced again. She found out that her husband had been cheating on her for the past 5 years. Thankfully she is still living for the Lord. But 15 years was a lot of time to lose in the wrong marriage.

Generally Christians tend to be too passive in their search for a mate. We have spoken quite a bit about this so far. Having said that, we always need to beware of extremes. You do not want to jump all the way to the other extreme and become overly aggressive. You probably need to be more proactive than you presently are, but don't be too aggressive otherwise you may end up forcing a relationship that isn't there.

It should be clear from what we have written in this book, that we do not believe in *"the one that God ordained for you."* We believe there are many members of the opposite sex who could potentially be good mates. But it is equally true that there are many people who could be bad mates. There are many people who could simply be wrong for you. You need to avoid them like the plague.

What is missionary dating?

Missionary dating is a term that means to treat a dating relationship like a mission field. A Christian dates an unsaved person, wins them to Christ in the process, then marries them. It sounds really straightforward on paper. Many Christian women feel they have to resort to this tactic because there are so few Christian men in churches.

I guess this would be the dating equivalent of starting your own business. Someone feels that there is too much competition for too few jobs, and someone else always ends up getting the job ahead of them. So they take matters into their own hands and they create their own source of income. Sometimes it works, sometimes it flops big time. In fact, most small businesses end in failure. People often take inspiration from the success stories of the few entrepreneurs who made it big. But statistically, most others will not enjoy the same success.

The same is true with missionary dating. You will always find someone who will tell you that they tried it and it worked. In fact, I have a good friend who is a pastor. While he was unsaved, he fell in love with a church girl, but he knew he had to convert. So he went through a superficial conversion just to impress her. But soon after, he received a genuine conviction from the Holy Spirit and got saved. They have been married for over 40 years now, and pastoring a church together.

Yet there are many others for whom it has not worked. They dated someone who took them for a ride. As the years went by, they felt like they travelled too far down that road to turn back. They end up wasting precious years chasing a relationship that was designed to elude them all along.

Someone recently wrote me stating that at age 40, she has finally realized that her boyfriend is not going to marry her. They had a child together a few years back, and because of this she did not want to marry anyone else. She kept believing God to cause the child's father to marry her. Years and years and years went by. Most likely he was playing the field, and never had any intention of marrying anyone. She practically wasted her youth on missionary dating. But I pray that she will still be able to find someone and live happily ever after. I sincerely wish that for her, but at the same time, we must learn from her mistakes.

The solution to one mistake is not a second mistake

Perhaps you are in a similar situation, where you have had a child outside of marriage. I am pretty sure the child is a great blessing from God. But how you got the child was clearly a sin and a mistake. I have absolutely no interest in judging you. We all have made mistakes. But the solution to one mistake is not a second mistake. Just because you have a child with someone out of wedlock is NOT a reason to marry that person. You could, but there is no rule that says you must. That person could be the embodiment of another mistake.

Susan found herself unmarried and pregnant at age 20. Her parents insisted that her boyfriend marry her and make an honest woman out of her. You know how the story goes. So said, so done. Her wedding was a dream, but her marriage has turned out to be a living nightmare. Her husband physically abuses her, she is clinically depressed, and she even attempted suicide once. Wouldn't it have been so much better had her parents not insisted on them getting married? Wouldn't she have been much better off as a single mom? The solution to one mistake is not a second mistake.

Be not unequally yoked

One of the gravest dangers of missionary dating is that you end up getting married to an unsaved person that you think is a Christian. You are way too personally and emotionally invested in the relationship to think objectively and clearly.

Cassidy dated and married an unsaved guy. At least that's how it appears to everyone else, but Cassidy doesn't see it that way. She believes that her husband is a *"secret Christian."* According to her this means that he is a Christian but he does not go to church or live a Christian life. When one of her friends questioned the concept of a secret Christian, Cassidy promptly ended the friendship with that faithless friend. It seems as though she wanted to be married so badly that she convinced herself of this. A secret Christian is a concept that cannot possibly be in accordance with sound Biblical doctrine. A secret Christian is another name for an unbeliever.

The Bible tells us in two places that Christians should marry other genuine Christians.

> *... she is at liberty to be married to whom she wishes, only in the Lord ... (1 Corinthians 7:39)*

> *Do not be unequally yoked together with unbelievers. For what fellowship has righteousness with lawlessness? And what communion has light with darkness? ... (2 Corinthians 6:14)*

Note that there is nothing in the context of 2 Corinthians 6:14 that limits its application to marriage. That scripture is deliberately broad. Yes it can apply to marriage – marrying an unbeliever would definitely be considered being unequally yoked. But there are other things that could also constitute an unequal yoke.

The scripture goes on to say, *"What fellowship does light have with darkness?"* This means that any kind of fellowship would constitute an unequal yoke. In the Bible, fellowship does not mean friendship or togetherness. Fellowship means association or union via a common bond. So you can have fellowship with or be unequally yoked with an unbeliever even if you are not married to them. If you are merely friends with someone who is not a Christian, that does not mean you associate with them spiritually or that you associate with their sin. But if you date someone, that constitutes fellowship. That's an unequal yoke even if you are not married. If the person gets genuinely saved along the way, then you got lucky. Most of the times, that does not happen. And some of the times, they drag you down with them, and before you know it you are living an unchristian life and you don't even know how you got there. You are unequally yoked.

People do not change

The premise of missionary dating is that you can win someone to Christ by association. That premise is wrong. You do not win people to Christ by being in a romantic relationship with them. It is debatable whether you can even win someone to Christ by being friends with them. I'm sure you have many friends who love you and respect you, but they do not share your conviction that Jesus Christ is the only way, the truth, and the life. Your friendship is clearly not winning them to Christ. Why would you think dating someone is going to bring them to Christ? Remember Joseph fled from Potiphar's wife. He did not remain there and try to win her over with his righteousness. That wasn't going to happen.

People come to Christ when the Holy Spirit convicts them of sin after they hear the gospel of Jesus Christ. This conviction leads to godly sorrow, which leads to repentance, which draws them to Christ. The person responds by surrendering their life to Jesus Christ.

When you try to win someone to Christ by dating them, you end up forcing things too soon. Most likely they will pray the sinner's prayer. But the sinner's prayer is not even in the Bible, and the Bible certainly does not say that repeating this prayer causes anyone to get saved. Most likely, this person will pray the prayer just because they feel pressured by you to do so. Then when you see no fruit of the Spirit in their lives, you wonder if they backslid. No, they were never saved. They just prayed the sinner's prayer to make you happy.

I have another secret to share with you. People do not change. Unless they are saved through genuine conviction by the Holy Spirit and are brought to genuine repentance before God, they will never change. Missionary dating is based on the hope that someone will one day become the person that you want. Missionary dating is based on what the person might become rather than who the person is. Would you like it if someone did that to you?

If you do not romantically like someone as they presently are, then don't date them. Most people carry the same weaknesses with them throughout their life. That's just a reality. They are not going to change into what you want them to be. The great Apostle Peter always had a problem with fear. He ran away when Jesus was being crucified. When he was walking in the Spirit, he learned to be bold. But even after he had the Holy Spirit, he still reverted to his old fearful ways (see Galatians 2:12). If you can't marry someone as they presently are, then you should never marry them.

By all means, you can work together with someone to iron out your flaws and improve yourselves. But don't make this change a requirement for marrying someone. Make it a project that you do together so that you both can grow together.

Betty was convinced that Matthew was the one for her, but Matthew was not saved. She believed that God had created him for her and he would eventually get saved. They started dating in their late teens and dated for 8 years while she waited for him to come to Christ. She put a lot of pressure on him to conform to a Christian life. This as you know is not something you can do easily if you are not saved. It therefore made Matthew very unhappy but he tried because he was in love with her. Eventually she gave up and broke it off with him. By this time, most of the godly men in her circles were already married. It took Betty more than 10 years to finally get married to a Christian man. 20 years later, Matthew is still not a Christian.

"But I just know that XYZ is the guy for me and God is going to save him." If you believe God plans to save XYZ and plans for you to get married to him, why not ask God to save him before you get involved with him? Why get your emotions involved and block out other potential persons while you wait for God to save him? There is nothing wrong with being friends with XYZ while you wait for and even fast and pray for God to save him. I dare say that your walk with God and your prayers will be all the more effective if you are not battling with requests from an unsaved boyfriend for sexual intimacy and at the very least being unequally yoked.

God never intended for marriage or courtship to be your mission field. And let's face it, when you are constantly trying to evangelize in your relationship, it puts a strain on things. It kills the romance. It prevents you from being real with them about your daily Christian walk. It also has the effect of placing so much pressure on the person being evangelized that it can make them very unhappy in the relationship. It can also make them feel that you consider them to not be good enough. Dating an unsaved person is a pull and tug. Your idea of a date is to go to the church BBQ. Their idea of a date may be to go clubbing. You don't want to compromise your faith but it is selfish to ask your unsaved partner to constantly choose what you want to do. How long can this last? Until they get saved? And what if they don't? How much time would you have wasted?

Missionary dating is not advisable. It is more likely to cause you to waste your life chasing something that is designed to elude you. As soon as you realize you are in a relationship where you are waiting for the other person to change or trying to make them change, it is time to walk away.

Being in the wrong relationship for too long

There is a song that says *"It is hard to belong to someone else when the right one comes along."* It's not a gospel song, but there is a whole lot of wisdom contained in that one line. You don't want to be in the wrong relationship. The longer you remain in a relationship with someone, the more people begin to associate you as a couple. Then potential mates would most likely back off because they know you as *"Bobby's girl"* or whomever it is. It will be difficult for them to picture you as their husband or wife.

If you spend too much time dating one specific person, then you develop a dependence on that person, which will pose a serious problem if you end up marrying someone else. If the only preparation you had for marriage was becoming attached to one specific person, then you are doing an injustice to the person you marry if that person turns out to be someone else. You will also be doing an injustice to yourself by wasting too much time with the wrong person.

One girl told me that she wishes she could get back all the time she wasted on her ex and use it to learn a language or pursue a degree. Or even better, in prayer and Bible study. Time is the only resource on this earth we can never get back. Don't waste it and then have regrets.

Being in too many wrong relationships

I recall an elderly unmarried woman once saying to me, *"Even a bad a relationship is better than no relationship."* I humbly beg to differ. When I was single I used to call some guys *"20s guys."* These were the kinds of guys you would be excused for marrying if you were in your early 20s and still unwise. After a certain age, we should have wisdom to avoid persons with fatal flaws. We are too wise to wait our whole lives for Prince Harry to dump Meghan Markle and come knocking on our door. But do not set about a whole life's journey with someone you just settled for because no one good was coming along.

There is an episode of *"How I met your mother"* about a minor character called Maggie. The main character Ted had always liked her, but Maggie was never single long enough for him to make a move. She would be in a relationship for years, then as soon as it broke up, within minutes to hours she would be back in another long term relationship.

That kind of life is well suited to a sitcom or to someone who is not interested in getting married. If you are interested in getting married, then you would not want to be like Maggie. There is nothing to gain from relationship hopping. You only need to be in one relationship. Your time is much better spent working on yourself.

Relationship experience counts for nothing

Another danger with being in the wrong relationship for too long or having too many wrong relationships is that it is really bad preparation for marriage. The best preparation for marriage is NOT relationship experience. It is what you do during your single time.

I once overheard a conversation between a pastor's wife and a single woman. The single woman was being propositioned by a male friend, but the pastor's wife did not think he was a good candidate. *"He is single yes, but he is 40 years old and has never been married."* "But 40 years is not that old", someone else interjected. The pastor's wife then reiterated, *"Yeah, but he NEVER GOT MARRIED."*

I could not believe what I was hearing. The pastor's wife was discrediting this guy because he was never married. Let's dissect that statement. She was implying that having been previously married or having lots of relationship experience is how you determine who will be a good husband or wife. Really? Am I the only person who thinks that logic is horribly flawed?

Do you know what is ironic? People like this pastor's wife would have no problem if the guy was previously married but now divorced. In her mind, being formerly married meant that since another woman determined that he was marriage material, then he is a better catch than the guy who was never in a long-term relationship. As far as the Bible is concerned, the fact that he is divorced is more significant than any marriage experience he might have. It is comprehensive proof that he does NOT know how to make a marriage work.

I am not trying to knock people who are divorced. I know that many people are divorced because they were innocently the victim of unfaithfulness or abuse on the part of their husband or wife. But it is also a fact that these experiences can result in a lot of trust issues and other related baggage. It is also a fact that very often infidelity is the result of unresolved deficiencies in a marriage relationship. People who are divorced need to stop thinking that they are saints while everyone else is evil. They need to seriously examine themselves to determine what they might have done wrong and what they can do better next time.

The best preparation for marriage is not having been previously married or being in a long term relationship. The best preparation is what you do during your single time. Your single life is supposed to prepare you for married life. Depending on how you spend your single life, you can develop certain attitudes that will go a long way in determining how good a husband or wife you will be.

One study has found that the likelihood of getting divorced decreases slightly for every sibling a person has. The reason for this is that growing up with siblings further the development of social skills useful in navigating marriage. In other words, it teaches you early in life how to live with other people – especially those who are really annoying.

This is interesting because modern society tends to look down on men who still live with their parents. Men absolutely must develop independence from their parents as they grow older. But too much independence is not necessarily a good thing. For one, if you get too independent for too long, it becomes difficult to transition into marriage. Living with your family goes a long way in teaching invaluable life skills. These skills are much more important to a marriage than relationship experience and independence.

Dating while you are vulnerable

Ana was just 12 when her grandmother died. Her grandmother was the only parent she had ever known, so she felt lost and devastated. Not long after the funeral, Peter (19) turned up in her life. Peter seemed to understand her and believe in her dreams. It seemed Peter was just what God had sent her to get through this difficult period. Peter systematically blocked out all other guys from her life. He told her that God had chosen her to be his wife. They later got married and what was an emotionally abusive courtship turned into a physically abusive and adulterous marriage. He eventually left her for another woman. Ana is now in her 40s and she is still suffering the negative effects of the aftermath of this relationship.

Petra was in her early 30s and going through the hardest time of her life. She felt she had no one to turn to and was having panic attacks and had to take sleeping tablets just to get through this difficult period. It was then that Larry came into her life. It felt as though he was just what she needed to get through this period. She quickly became emotionally dependent on him. What followed was a tumultuous abusive relationship which caused her to waste 9 of her childbearing years on a dead-end endeavor.

Stories such as these abound. I have heard so many of them that it makes me sick. It seems that the devil specializes in sending people with fatal flaws into the lives of children of God when we are most vulnerable. He knows that it would be easy at such a time for these people to prey on you. The ultimate aim of the devil here is to destroy or at least delay your destiny. Don't be ignorant of his wiles. Guard your heart and your life especially when you are vulnerable. Not everyone who seems to be God-sent is truly a blessing. God also sends people to help us during difficult times but we need to be wise and discerning.

How to identify a true Christian

If you must marry a fellow Christian, then it is imperative that you be able to identify a Christian when you see one. The more mature you are in the Lord, the easier this is. But there are some church-folk / church-goers / church-members who are not necessarily saved. They may even be in ministry, and they may appear to be very spiritual. They may come highly recommended by their pastors and may even claim to exercise spiritual gifts. None of these things mean that they are genuinely saved.

Christians are supposed to know for sure (100%) that they are saved and in Christ.

> *These things I have written to you who believe in the name of the Son of God, that you may know that you have eternal life, and that you may continue to believe in the name of the Son of God. ... (1 John 5:13)*

However, although you can be 100% percent sure of your own salvation, you cannot be 100% sure of someone else's salvation. But you can be 99% sure. And that's good enough.

We are told that if you believe in your heart that Jesus Christ is Lord, and confess the Lord Jesus Christ, you are saved.

> *... if you confess with your mouth the Lord Jesus and believe in your heart that God has raised Him from the dead, you will be saved. ... For "whoever calls on the name of the Lord shall be saved." ... (Romans 10:9,13)*

However, the problem with confession is that it can be faked.

> *Not everyone who says to Me, 'Lord, Lord,' shall enter the kingdom of heaven, but he who does the will of My Father in heaven ... (Matthew 7:21)*

Romans 10 places the emphasis on heart belief. Verbal confession should be the result of genuine faith. But there are many people who go to church and *"identify"* as Christians without having genuine faith. This means that they tick *"Christian"* when filling out a form. But that is the full extent of their faith. They are merely professing Christians. So how do you know when someone is merely saying the right words without having the right condition of their heart?

To complicate matters, even genuine Christians are very imperfect. We still have the flesh (old sinful nature) to deal with, and because of this, we sin often. We all fall short daily. In Romans 7:24, Paul said, *"Oh wretched man that I AM"* not *"Oh wretched man that I WAS."* So you can't look at everyone's flaws and judge if they are saved. That would be judging unfairly. We all have flaws.

So how can you identify a true Christian? Let us consider two theological words associated with salvation – sanctification and regeneration.

After you are saved, God begins a process in you called sanctification where He gradually cleanses your heart. It is a gradual process which comes to a completion on that day when you are glorified (when you get to heaven). In other words, you will not achieve sinless perfection in this life. Sanctification is gradual, therefore you cannot judge a Christian by their level of sanctification. We all have a different level of sanctification.

Regeneration however, happens the moment you are saved. It is instantaneous. It results in us being dramatically changed from an old creature to a new creation. This is what you need to look for. The evidence of regeneration is a changed life. Not a perfect life, but a changed one. So you are not looking for sinless perfection, but evidence of a transformation.

Here are some tests to know if you (or someone else) have had a genuine salvation experience.

1) You find that there is an inexplicable love for others in you that wasn't there before.

   No one has seen God at any time. If we love one another, God abides in us, and His love has been perfected in us. … (1 John 4:12)

2) You have a sudden urge to obey God and live righteously.

   Now by this we know that we know Him, if we keep His commandments. … (1 John 2:3)

   In this the children of God and the children of the devil are manifest: Whoever does not practice righteousness is not of God, nor is he who does not love his brother. … (1 John 3:10)

The obvious corollary is that if someone is living in open sin and deliberate unrighteousness, there is a strong chance that person is not saved. If someone does not display some kind of change where the person now has a desire to live for God and to follow Christ, then that person merely prayed the sinner's prayer. They confessed Jesus, but they don't have genuine faith in their hearts ... yet.

You can't presume to pronounce judgment on that person since you don't know with 100% certainty what their heart condition is, but you can choose to not marry them.

Avoid certain *"Christians"* as well

In addition to avoiding fake Christians, there are many Christians who may not be good for you. It could be that they are living very carnal lives, or they are not ready for marriage. There are a lot of qualities that could raise red flags that trouble lies ahead. Here are some of the red flags the Bible warns us to look out for and avoid.

People in the church who are immoral

> *I wrote to you in my epistle not to keep company with sexually immoral people. Yet I certainly did not mean with the sexually immoral people of this world, or with the covetous, or extortioners, or idolaters, since then you would need to go out of the world. But now I have written to you <u>not to keep company with anyone named a brother</u>, who is sexually immoral, or covetous, or an idolater, or a reviler, or a drunkard, or an extortioner – <u>not even to eat with such a person</u>. ... (1 Corinthians 5:9-11)*

People who are deceptive and self-serving

> *Now I urge you, brethren, note those who cause divisions and offenses, contrary to the doctrine which you learned, and <u>avoid them</u>. For those who are such do not serve our Lord Jesus Christ, but their own belly, and by smooth words and flattering speech deceive the hearts of the simple ... (Romans 16:17-18)*

People with unsound doctrines and spooky weird beliefs

> *If anyone teaches otherwise and does not consent to wholesome words, even the words of our Lord Jesus Christ, and to the doctrine which accords with godliness, he is proud, knowing nothing, but is obsessed with disputes and arguments over words, from which come envy, strife, reviling, evil suspicions, useless wranglings of men of corrupt minds and destitute of the truth, who*

suppose that godliness is a means of gain. <u>From such withdraw yourself</u>. ... (1 Timothy 6:3-5)

People with legalistic doctrines

Beware of dogs, beware of evil workers, beware of the mutilation! ... (Philippians 3:2)

Disorderly people who do not walk the Christian walk

But we command you, brethren, in the name of our Lord Jesus Christ, that you <u>withdraw from every brother</u> who walks disorderly and not according to the tradition which he received from us. ... (2 Thessalonians 3:6)

People who are lazy or will not work

For even when we were with you, we commanded you this: If anyone will not work, neither shall he eat. ... (2 Thessalonians 3:10)

Spiritual people who are not godly

For men will be lovers of themselves, lovers of money, boasters, proud, blasphemers, disobedient to parents, unthankful, unholy, unloving, unforgiving, slanderers, without self-control, brutal, despisers of good, traitors, headstrong, haughty, lovers of pleasure rather than lovers of God, having a form of godliness but denying its power. And <u>from such people turn away!</u> ... (2 Timothy 3:2-5)

What about people who are divorced?

Many Christians are divorced or are in relationships with people who are divorced, and they are not sure how to proceed. In our website bibleissues.org, there is an article outlining in detail what the Bible teaches about divorce and remarriage. I will outline the main ideas here.

- When two people are married, it is God who joins them together.
- God only considers the marriage dissolved if one of them dies or if they divorce because of infidelity. In such cases, they are free to remarry.
- If the divorce took place for any other reason, regardless of what the law of the land allows, God considers them to still be married. As far as GOD is concerned, their *"divorce"* – although legal – is merely a separation and not a dissolution of the marriage. For this reason, if they get remarried under such circumstances, God considers it adultery.
- Here is where it gets complicated. If during this *"separation"*, one party has an affair or gets (re)married, then God would consider that to be

adultery, and we are back to square one. That would mean the dissolution of the marriage, and they are free to remarry.

So if you are widowed, you are free to remarry. If you are divorced because of infidelity OR your ex is now remarried OR your ex subsequently had an affair, then you are free to remarry. If however, you are divorced and there was never any infidelity in your marriage AND you ex is still single and available, then I believe the Bible requires you to remain single or be reconciled, not remarry. This is my understanding of the divorce and remarriage teachings in the Bible.

Do not ignore red flags

Mae met Al in church. Al was involved in altar ministry and intercession. He claimed to have a number of spiritual gifts in which he operated. Within one month of dating, he was proposing to her constantly. She considered it but felt she needed more time. By the 5th week of their relationship, he asked her *"What would you do if when we are married, God told me to leave my job?"* This got her thinking about his intentions. She quickly realized that he was seeing her as a cash cow since she was a doctor. His desire to marry her quickly was because of a desire to be financially secure. On top of that she realized that even during their 6 week courtship, he was being unfaithful to her. Even though she was in her late 30s and anxious to get married, she did not ignore the warning signs.

Sarah met Marlon at a get together at the house of a mutual friend. The attraction was instant and strong. They immediately started chatting for hours on the phone, and soon started seeing each other. It all seemed perfect on paper. They were both Christians, and had mutual friends. He was an engineer and she was an accountant. He said and did all the right things. Somehow she still had a doubt in her mind. Something about him reminded her of an uncle who had sexually abused her as a child. There was nothing tangible, just a feeling. Eventually she burst out with it one day, and he confessed that he had sexually abused one of his infant cousins. She prayed with him but refused to get into a dating relationship with him. He insisted he was reformed, but she just did not believe it. He eventually got married and was divorced within 5 years. His wife was admitted for psychiatric treatment as the result of the mental and emotional abuse she had suffered at his hands.

If someone gets angry too quickly or is a chronic liar, that could signal trouble ahead. If someone is abusive – physically, mentally or emotionally – that is a major red flag. Too many Christians make the mistake of putting up with abusive behavior hoping the abusive person will change. Physical abuse is one of those areas where people simply do not change. This is one area where you should adopt a one-strike policy. Respect yourself and exit a relationship at the first instance of abuse.

Be open to God's guidance

People will always show you who they are if you are willing to be observant. Don't be blinded by love or desperation. Keep God's Word in your heart – it will come in handy when you need it. Also remain open to God's guidance and leading. Don't go trying to hear God's voice or making up revelations, but IF God shows you something, then take heed. Just remember, you may not always like what God might say to you.

Once when I was single, I met a guy who looked like a potential Christian husband. On the surface, he had a lot of the characteristics I was looking for, but I felt as though God was saying, *"Google him."* The first thing that came up in the search was an image of him in a prison outfit. He had actually served time for pedophilia.

I recall another time when one of my best friends was dating what seemed to be the perfect guy. However, whenever I prayed about their relationship, I would always get a vision of the guy with an ugly evil looking head instead of his own head. I tried to tell my friend to be careful but she was in love. Finally I started praying for God to cause him to reveal his true self to my friend. He soon showed himself to be very cruel. We later found out that he was involved in the illegal drug trade and his successful business was just a money laundering front.

Don't settle

We know that Ruth did not wait for Boaz, she was very proactive in making things happen. But at the same time, she did not spend her single time relationship hopping. There is a great quote I would like to share with you. The part about Ruth waiting for Boaz – just take that in context and appreciate the main point the author is trying to make.

While you are waiting on your Boaz, don't settle for any of his relatives: Broke-az, Po-az, Lyin-az, Cheating-az, Dumb-az, Drunk-az, Cheap-az, Lockedup-az, Goodfornothing-az, Lazy-az, and especially his third cousin, Beatinyo-az. Wait on your Boaz and make sure he respects Yoaz.

… Author unknown

MYTH #8

MISUNDERSTANDING THE ROLE OF PARENTS

In this chapter

We will learn about the proper place for parents in your marriage decision. Do you absolutely need their consent? Do you have other parent issues you need to sort out? How else can parents help or hinder you in your search?

Chapter outline

- Horror stories
- Do you need your parents' consent?
- What if your parents don't consent?
- Proper role for parents
- What about arranged marriages?
- Be aware of your parents' flaws
- Heal any broken relationships

Horror stories

Maria moved to Canada from Jamaica with her husband and daughter. But afterward, Maria's father, who lives in Jamaica, became ill. So Maria made a decision to go back to her home country to tend to her father, while her husband and daughter continued their life in North America. That was 7 years ago. Maria is still in Jamaica caring for her ailing dad – 7 years apart from her husband and daughter.

What are your thoughts on that? Did Maria do the right thing? Did she do the wrong thing? Was there another course of action she should have taken? Was she supposed to leave and cleave? Or would she have been worse than an infidel if she had abandoned her sick father?

Isabela left Central America to move to the United States together with her parents and her brother when she was a child. They were fleeing an oppressive regime in their home country. It was a battle to build a life for themselves. They constantly had to face fears of being deported. But after a long and grueling struggle, they were granted refugee status and later became American citizens. They went through a lot together.

But now, after having provided a great new life for Isabela, her parents won't let go. Isabela is now well qualified and has a fairly high paying job. But Isabela cannot seem to find a husband. She has had a number of relationships, but every time her parents would disapprove. Unfortunately, their approval is vital to Isabela. She has this dream of her father walking her down the aisle, but he refuses to let her go. They depend on her financially, and they are afraid that if she gets married, they would have to find a new place to live and a new source of income.

What is Isabela supposed to do? Get married without her parents' consent? Sacrifice herself for her parents' happiness? After all, they sacrificed so much for her. It is a tough decision.

Neil recently graduated from a theological seminary. He is in a relationship, hoping to get married soon, but his girlfriend's parents do not approve of him. Further, his church is hesitant to allow him into the ministry because they have a policy against single men being in ministry. What is Neil supposed to do? He seems to be stuck unless he gets his in-laws' permission to marry their daughter.

All of these are examples where marriages or potential marriages are in trouble because of parents. On one hand, you don't want to show ingratitude to the people who raised you and sacrificed so much for you. But on the other hand, you can't allow them to steal your future. Will Smith's character on the *Fresh Prince of Bel Air* once said, *"My mom gave me life, and she can take it back."* What do you do when parents (whom you love and respect) are standing in the way of your marriage?

Do you need your parents' consent?

In the ideal scenario, the approval of your parents and pastors is invaluable. Usually, these individuals possess a lot of wisdom and can see things that people who are blinded by love cannot see. But what about the rare cases where they are not being reasonable?

In the Bible (especially the Old Testament), when a man was interested in a woman, he had to request permission from her parents, give them a dowry, and then they would give him their daughter. When Jacob met Rachel, he loved her, but her father's price was 7 years of labor. Jacob happily did this because of his love for Rachel.

This was the practice in the Old Testament. But it is noteworthy, that this is not necessarily what God commanded of us. Many Old Testament commands were given merely to ratify whatever culture or custom existed at the time. For example, when a man died without having children, his brother was supposed to marry his widow and have children for him. I know this sounds weird and borderline perverted to modern-day folk, but God actually killed one person for violating that command. Seriously, God killed him for not impregnating his sister-in-law. That sounds like something out of a reality TV show. This command was not God's design, but simply the cultural norm of the time.

In these olden times, women were the property of their fathers. That is why she had to be given in marriage. Then the ownership was transferred from her father to her husband. I know your feminist blood is probably boiling over right now, but that's how it was.

I would say things have changed a wee bit since then. Today women are much more independent. Nobody owns them. Once children come of age, they are no longer dependent on their parents. As a result of this, parental permission is not a prerequisite for marriage, but it sure would be nice. It would be desirable. It would be ideal. But it is not an absolute necessity.

In the majority of cases, parents have the best interest of their children at heart, so they do what is needed to ensure that they marry good people. In most cases, parental consent carries a lot of weight. If you have parents who genuinely care about your best interest, they may be able to spot things in your boyfriend or girlfriend that you may be blinded to. It is usually best to trust their wisdom.

But in a minority of cases, there are problems with parents. In some cases the parents oppose a potential marriage for no good reason. In other cases, they interfere after the marriage has already taken place. It is truly sad when parents raise a child and bring them to a point in life where they can marry and move on with their own life, but then refuse to let go.

What does the Bible teach us to do in situations like this?

> *Therefore a man shall leave his father and mother and be joined to his wife, and they shall become one flesh ... (Genesis 2:24)*
>
> *Honor your father and your mother, that your days may be long ... (Exodus 20:12)*
>
> *But if any widow has children or grandchildren, let them first learn to show piety at home and to repay their parents; for this is good and acceptable before God ... But if anyone does not provide for his own, and especially for those of his household, he has denied the faith and is worse than an infidel ... (1 Timothy 5:4,8)*

The 1 Timothy 5 passage teaches that we are to support our parents and grandparents if required. Those who don't do that are worse than an infidel. Thus we are to honor them. But at the same time, when we must get married, we are told to leave parents and cleave to our husband or wife.

Clearly it is a very delicate balance. Ideally there should be no conflict at all between these two requirements, but unfortunately, some Christians find themselves smack in the middle of this conflict.

We have an obligation to our husband/wife, to our children, as well as to our parents and grandparents. But which one takes precedence in the case of a conflict? Clearly your immediate family – husband/wife and children. They are your main priority, followed by parents and grandparents.

What if your parents don't consent?

So what should you do if your parents are standing in the way of you getting married? Firstly you should consider whether they have genuine reasons for objecting. Most parents are very wise and oftentimes can spot potential dangers that you may be blinded to. If their reason for objecting to a relationship is valid, then take heed.

Sandra should have taken heed to her parents. She was beautiful, and Aaron was an admirer who wanted a serious relationship with her. However, she had several admirers. She found Wesley to be more exciting. He had a nice car, he took her dancing, he had a great job, he was older. But he was selfish and treated her badly. She failed to realize that Aaron was the better choice. He was not as exciting, he came from a poor family and drove an old car. But he was fun, caring and selfless. He was busy studying for his medical degree and now has a great career. Sandra's family had begged her to give Aaron a chance and to break up with Wesley. But she did not pay them any heed. Her relationship with Wesley eventually came to a bitter end. She regrets it now because she realizes that Aaron was one in a million. But it is too late. Aaron now has a lovely family and continues to be a kind hearted and solid person.

But if the parents' reason for objecting is not valid, then you have a decision to make. I know one mother who boycotted 4 out of 5 of her children's weddings because she did not approve. Wow! I think it's safe to say she has some control issues.

People write me all the time through our website bibleissues.org asking what to do if parents don't approve. One guy told me that his girlfriend's parents don't approve of him, and she won't get married without their consent. But they have been in love with each other for the past 4 years. So I quizzed him a little.

Me: Why did it take you so long to ask her parents' permission?

Him: I first asked her father 4 years ago and he told me to wait. But during this time, we fell in love. I kept asking his permission many other times, and his answer has now changed to no.

Me: Are her parents always this way?

Him: Yes, they have a history of being this way for as long as I can remember. They are good people but they are very controlling.

Me: Is there anything about you that gives them reason to object?

Him: Other than the fact that I am a different race, I can't think of anything.

Me: Is there any chance your girlfriend will marry you without her parents' consent?

Him: She insists that she must have their consent.

Me: How old is she?

Him: 21.

Me: What does your pastor think?

Him: He insists that I must get her parents' approval.

Me: Well you basically have 3 options – convince them, convince her, or walk. It is either you convince her parents to give you permission, you convince your girlfriend to marry without their consent, or you walk away.

He eventually decided he had no choice but to move on. I told him,

> *In my opinion, that was the best decision. The real issue here is not her parents (who sound unreasonable from your side of the story). The real issue is your girlfriend. If at age 21, she still acts like a child, you are better off without her. You would have had a lot of problems anyway being married to someone like that. Her father would always be first in her life, never you. They would interfere any chance they get. Go in peace.*

I know of another similar case where the parents objected and refused to give permission. The couple felt they had no choice but to elope. They secretly got married without any ceremony, without any permission. The parents were livid when they found out. They were also very upset with their pastor for not taking their side. The pastor addressed the congregation the next Sunday on that issue. He lambasted the parents and other such parents for forcing their children into that situation. He said,

> *I have seen these kids grow up in church. They have served God faithfully since their youth. Now they are grown up and want to get married like normal people. And it's a case of two Christians marrying each other. Why would you deny them the joy of having their father walk them down the aisle and give them away? Why would you deny them that joy?*

Today, that particular couple has been married for nearly 20 years and still in love. You need to honor your parents, but when it is time to go, leave and cleave. Further, giving priority to your new family (husband, wife and children) does not stand in opposition to honoring your parents. You can do both.

Proper role for parents

Parents have a crucial role to play in raising godly children – training them in the way they should go. But once they come of age, they must learn to let go. In some cases, parents have been known to meddle a little too much.

There is an old sitcom called Cheers with a character called Cliff who is the classic mama's boy. When at thirty-something he finally met a woman he liked, he decided to take his mother to meet her. His mother took one deep gulp and said in a slow deliberate old-lady voice, *"Well, I guess I should meet the person you have chosen to replace me."*

In the Old Testament, instead of standing in the way of their children getting married, we actually see parents actively looking for husbands and wives for their children. The best known example is of Abraham looking for a wife for Isaac, which we have talked about earlier in the book.

So a parent's job is not to raise children so they can hold on to them, but rather raise them so they can release them into society. Instead of being threatened when their kids get married, parents should be very much active in helping their kids get married. This does not have to be weird. Parents and the wider community can play a role in helping their children find husbands and wives.

Katelynn (a member of our Bible Issues Facebook group) shared how parents played a positive role in her relationship and eventual marriage to Blayne. She met Blayne when his younger brother married her friend. The fact that Blayne's younger brother married before him made him a little depressed. So he took to Facebook and posted something to that effect.

Katelynn read his post and thought to herself, *"Hmmm."* She decided to be proactive without being overly assertive. She commented on his post, *"Don't worry, you will find someone, in Jesus' name."* And she left it in God's hand because she had made a decision to make God – and not the pursuit of a husband – the center of her world.

Then his parents saw her comment and encouraged him to ask Katelynn out. So he invited her to a family game night. After that they started seeing each other more, they visited each other's churches, and recently got married. Katelynn knew this was a godly union because it helped her relationship with God to grow exponentially.

This is a great example of being proactive and trusting God at the same time. It is also a great example of how parents can play a positive role in helping their kids find husbands or wives.

What about arranged marriages?

You have probably looked at our profile picture at the back of the book and thought to yourself, *"What do they know about looking for a mate? They were probably engaged since they were babies."* Believe it or not, neither of us has ever been to India. We grew up in Trinidad in the Caribbean in a society that does not have arranged marriages – at least not in our generation. I must admit however, there were times we wished we could have had an arranged marriage because that would have made the whole process infinitely easier.

What about arranged marriages? Does the Bible say anything about it? Is this a good idea or a bad idea?

We must first of all appreciate that the term *"arranged marriage"* has different meanings. A long time ago in countries like India, two sets of parents would meet while their children were babies and promise them to each other. When the children grew up, they then got married to the one that was promised to them. That is one form of arranged marriages.

But not everyone had that *"luxury"* of being promised that early in life. Some of them grew up without having any promised mate. But when they were of age, their parents would meet other parents of eligible partners, and they would arrange the marriage. The children who were about to get married would meet each other for the first time on their wedding day.

Today that no longer happens – not even in India. Arranged marriages have evolved slightly. Parents would still meet to help locate potential partners for their children. Then they would give their children the opportunity to meet these potential partners under supervised conditions. After the first meeting, the children would decide if they liked each other, and if so, they would get engaged. The major difference now is that the children actually have a choice in the matter. This is the modern form of arranged marriages.

With arranged marriages, you don't fall in love and then wait for a proposal. You get married, and then *"love comes later."* That's the philosophy of it. People in those countries (including Christian theologians) scoff at the idea of a *"love-marriage"* where people must fall in love before they get married. Of course that is their culture.

In the West, people typically meet, fall in love, propose, and then get married. But the statistics are quite interesting. 39% of married couples meet their significant other through friends in common while 18% meet at work. This mean 57% of people get married to people who are part of their social network. So even in the West, there is a significant percentage of people who meet their significant other through common friends, family and associates.

This is not very different from the modern form of arranged marriages. The whole idea of having to go out there in the meat market and cold-approach strangers with pickup lines – only 22% of people find their husband or wife that way.

Based on that information, we don't have to totally scoff at the idea of an arranged marriage. I know it is embarrassing when friends and parents introduce you to other single people, but that is not necessarily a bad thing. In fact, you are statistically more likely to find a marriage partner that way than any other way.

So by all means, use your friends and family to help you in your search. I am sure they would be eager to help. Even my wife Indira fancies herself as a matchmaker. She loves to try to match-up her single friends with each other. You have absolutely nothing to lose by meeting someone. The more people you meet, the more likely you are to find someone you really like.

Be aware of your parents' flaws

There are other ways parents can affect or influence the marriage of their children. They can be directly involved in a good or bad way, as we have discussed earlier. But they can also be indirectly involved.

Have you ever observed the phenomenon of women marrying someone who is almost identical to their fathers? Or men marrying wives who remind them of their mothers? The reason for this is that children tend to develop the same attitudes and preferences their parents have. Human beings tend to gravitate to the familiar therefore they subconsciously choose partners who will allow them to maintain continuity in their existing way of life. As a result they end up being just like their parents – liking the same things and the same types of people.

This could be a good thing or a bad thing depending on your specific situation. If your father was a player, you would want to try extra hard not to end up marrying another player. If your mom was a control freak, you may wish to be aware of that so you avoid making the same mistake yourself.

A lot of what people call generational curses are really self-fulfilling prophecies and learned behavior. Instead of breaking some fictitious curse, we simply need to be aware of these behaviors and make a decision to avoid them. We need to be aware of our parents' shortcomings, and learn to overcome them.

Pamela's father was an alcoholic, unfaithful to her mother and physically abusive. Pamela married Jim who had the same characteristics as her father. Early in the abusive marriage, Jim walked out. Her family was actually relieved that she was now free. But shortly thereafter, she got into another relationship. The second guy was also physically abusive. He would apologize and then be abusive again cyclically. In one instance, the abuse was so bad, Pamela fled the house in fear for her life. Pamela has ended up just like her mother, and needs serious counseling to end this cycle.

Perhaps you have similar issues. Your father was abusive or absent. Maybe the only memories you have of him are negative. Perhaps your mother was controlling and manipulative. It is imperative that you identify these things honestly and openly, otherwise you will take them into any relationship you have.

Heal any broken relationships

You should consider your relationship with your parents and siblings to be training for your future relationship with your husband or wife. For many single Christians unfortunately, this has gone horrendously wrong. If it is possible, take the initiative to heal any broken relationship with your family before you get married. If you hold bitterness and unforgiveness toward them, then you may end up taking this with you into your marriage. If you haven't spoken to your father in years, pick up the phone today. This simple exercise will go such a long way in helping you to develop relationship handling skills that will be invaluable after you're married.

In our first book, *"small devil, BIG GOD"*, we shared the testimony of someone we called Jenna. Jenna's father left when she was 4 years old. Jenna cried for weeks for her daddy. But over time she learned to cope by being tough. She grew very cynical of men. At age 19, Jenna got saved. She had a lot of difficulty with the concept of a heavenly Father, because in her mind, a father was not a good person. But God began to soften her heart and she learned to cry out to God and cast her cares on Him. As she yielded herself to Him, God gradually took away all the bitterness and pain from her heart. Jenna was actually able to call her father and forgive him.

Today Jenna is married to someone who is not like her father. Her husband loves her tremendously and cherishes her. And Jenna is an excellent wife, who no longer carries around the baggage associated with being from a broken home.

You can do all things through Christ who strengthens you. You can deal with the baggage you may have through the power of God at work in you. Don't think that getting married will solve these problems. Take the initiative and deal with them first. You will reap the dividends after you get married.

YOUR ACTION PLAN

When waiting seems painful

Let's be realistic, it can hurt to see your younger friends and relatives getting married while you sit on the proverbial shelf. Well-meaning people offer advice while cruel people scoff at you, and to be honest you are not sure which hurts more.

This is not how you envisioned your life. By this time you surely thought you would be taking your children to Sunday school and complaining about sleepless nights with babies crying. But instead you wait for love. You look for love in vain. You try to put on a brave face when it hurts. I remember having to call my pastor and cry after a particularly cruel comment by a relative. How do you cope?

First having read this book, I encourage you to allow it to minister to you and then take any action you need to take. Whether it be putting a gorgeous photo of yourself on eHarmony, or starting a journey of emotional healing … just do it. Don't wait another day.

Throughout this book, we have shared Biblical principles to guide you in your search for a Christian husband or wife. We have debunked a lot of myths and wrong teachings that cause Christians to look for the wrong thing in the wrong way.

We pray that at this point, you would have been able to identify anything in your life that may be hindering you from finding a husband or wife. The purpose of this book is to provide scriptural guidance so that you trust God the right way and for the right thing, so that your hope is based on what God promised and not what some human tradition teaches.

We must avoid the temptation to be overly passive. We must learn to be proactive and yet trust God at the same time – not just proactive in finding a spouse, but proactive in working on yourself.

What are your reasons for wanting to get married?

- Companionship
- Finding a ministry helper

- Sex / intimacy
- Having a family / children

What are some things you need to work on?

- Emotional baggage
- Daddy issues
- Bad relationships
- Bad friendships
- Personality issues
- Unforgiveness / bitterness / resentment
- Selfishness / self-centeredness
- Unholiness in your Christian walk
- Getting your ex out of your life

What are some proactive things you can do to help you meet more eligible singles?

- Identify churches you can visit
- Identify persons who can introduce you to new friends
- Identify Christian co-workers who are members of other churches
- Identify ministries you can get involved in
- Set up profiles in various online dating sites / apps
- Find an older man, woman or couple to mentor you

Seasons change

If you have failed relationships in your past, I know they can seem to have a cumulative effect. Every failed relationship seems to take you closer to never finding someone to marry. We know the feeling. But it is only a feeling.

David (a member of our Bible Issues Facebook group) faced a similar situation. He had just come out of a breakup with a *"Christian"* girl who turned out to have been sleeping with his brother. So David surrendered all to God and actually gave up on getting married unless God made it obvious that He had other plans. Then through a couple who were mutual friends, he met Jodie, one of the worship singers in his church. They started talking and expressed interest in each other. The couple encouraged them and counseled them. They also got the blessings of their parents. They got married around the same time we completed this book. It took God six months to turn that derailing situation around.

If you are an older single Christian, I know the road may seem discouraging at times. You look at others who get married young and wonder why the same thing could not happen to you. But you still need to trust God while not neglecting to do your part. Just keep doing what you are supposed to do, stop doing what you are not supposed to do, and trust God to do what He promised to do. And most of all, don't give up.

You only need to succeed once

I remember watching a tennis match a few years ago – the Wimbledon final of 2001 – between Patrick Rafter and Goran Ivanisevic (don't try to pronounce it☺). Goran had tried unsuccessfully for years to win Wimbledon. Three times previously, he had reached the final only to lose in heartbreaking fashion. His last loss in 1998 was extremely painful. For years he was haunted by two errors he had made in that match that cost him his dream. He was never the same after that loss. And it seemed as though he was doomed to never win Wimbledon.

But in 2001, he reached the final once again, and was playing for a chance to achieve his elusive dream. The match was close and grueling. Late into the 5th and deciding set, Goran edged into the lead and was now serving for the Wimbledon championship. He dream was closer than it had ever been. All he needed to do was hold his nerve and win his final service game, and he would be champion.

Goran was in tears before the service game even began. He was overcome with emotion. He could barely compose himself to actually play tennis. If any ball came back on his side of the court, he simply did not have the frame of mind to handle it. His body was crippled with emotion. The only thing he could muster the strength to do was serve. On every point, he had to serve an ace or double-fault.

Finally, he was able to hold his nerve and win match point – and the tears poured out uncontrollably. At long last, Goran was a Wimbledon champion. He climbed into the crowd to hug his father, who was also in tears after witnessing his son finally succeed after so many years of failure.

Goran later said that his biggest fear was waking up the next morning knowing he lost Wimbledon again. But Goran knew that no matter how many times he had failed in the past, how many heartbreaks, how many almosts and maybes; all he needed to do was win Wimbledon once, and all would be forgotten.

This was something that comforted me during my difficult searching years when it seemed that every relationship was doomed to end in failure, and I was destined to never find what I was looking for. I knew that no matter how many times I tried before and failed, I only needed to succeed once. And in that moment, all the failures of the past – all the disappointments, the heartbreaks, the could-have-beens, the should-have-beens, and the would-have-beens – would all disappear into a distant oblivion, never to be remembered again. This is exactly what happened when Indira and I met.

There will always be another bus

I remember once I was trying to catch a bus only to see it pull off as I reached the bus stop. I had just missed it, but that was OK since the next bus should have only been 15 minutes away. 15 minutes, I could live with.

I waited on that bus stop bench for 2 hours. 2 hours in the Miami sun when buses were scheduled to pass every 15 minutes!

Occasionally, I would see something in the distance that looked like my bus, but every time, it turned out to be some other bus (someone else's bus) or a bus that was not in service (a bus that was not looking for passengers right now). Should I just give up and go home? Should I give up and call a taxi? But knowing my luck, the bus would show up 1 minute after I got into the taxi. I kept telling myself *"the bus will be here soon."*

This started to bear frightening similarity to my own search for a wife. When I was younger, it was not a big deal. I had time. But as the years caught up to me, it felt as though every failure was a step closer to never finding someone. Everyone I liked was either taken or unavailable for whatever reason. *"Should I just give up?"*

As 15 minutes turned into half-hour and approached 1 hour, I grew increasingly agitated as my anger with God reached a crescendo. If I had only arrived 1 minute earlier, I would have caught the bus and all of this could have been avoided. Why couldn't God just delay that bus by 1 minute? Why couldn't God just let the buses pass every 15 minutes like they were supposed to? Why did everything have to be so hard?

Then I felt as though God put these thoughts into my heart. *"Do you really think there will never be another bus? Do you think the bus you missed was the last bus that there ever will be?"* And immediately, I felt a sense a calm envelop me. I knew exactly what God was trying to communicate to me. It didn't matter how many relationships I had lost. It didn't matter how many times before I had failed. It didn't even matter how long I had been waiting. My last relationship was not the last eligible person I would ever meet. I only needed to succeed once, and instantly, all the failures of the past would be erased.

Waiting 2 hours for a bus in the Miami heat was never as pleasant as when God was patiently ministering to me and speaking words of assurance into my heart. Mind you, I still had to wait another hour before my bus came. But by this time, my entire demeanor had changed. All the frustration was gone. And when the next bus finally arrived, guess what happened. About three of them showed up at the same time.

You will go through seasons when nothing seems to go right. Everything that can go wrong will go wrong à la Murphy's law. During those times, stop trying and start crying out to God. Don't go looking for a relationship during this season. Just seek Him and find out what He wants to teach you. Let God minister to you and show you what He is trying to accomplish. Work on yourself and see how you can grow and become a better Christian. The season will change – and when it does you will be ready for it.

Against the odds

> *... for your love is better than wine ... (Song of Solomon 1:2)*

Denver and I agree that we have found a love that has changed our lives. A love that has positively impacted the essence of who we are. A love that has brought great joy. We found love against the odds.

I recall, when I was single, a minister speaking to me about a man of God who is searching for a mate and he will find me and treasure me. I recall smiling politely and thinking, *"There is no man of God looking for me so he can treasure me. This minister is well meaning but so very wrong."* It turns out he was right. I have been treated like a treasure by Denver every day since we met.

God is no respecter of persons. If we found love, so can you. I encourage you to shake off the past failures, past mistakes, and hold your head high as you embark on an exciting journey towards the love of a lifetime. Put what you have learned in this book to use and start this new phase of your life. Don't forget to send us an invitation. We look forward to dancing at your wedding.☺

ABOUT THE AUTHORS

4 truths and a lie about the authors

Can you identify the truth from the myth? 4 of these statements about us are true, and one is a myth. Go to www.8myths.com to get the answer.
1. I survived a shipwreck
2. I survived a tiger attack
3. I survived an abduction
4. I survived a train crash
5. I survived Hurricane Katrina

Dr. Denver Cheddie is Bible teacher and an Ordained Minister in the Church of God (*Headquartered in Cleveland, TN*). He is also an Associate Professor with a PhD in Mechanical Engineering. He holds Masters Degrees in Biblical Studies, Business Administration and Mechanical Engineering.

Indira Rampaul-Cheddie is a prayer warrior who operates in various gifts of the Spirit including healing and the word of knowledge. God uses her to provide comfort through counseling. By profession, she is an attorney-at-law. She holds Masters Degrees in Biblical Studies, Petroleum Law & Policy, and Business Administration.

We have been married since December 2010, and we share a vision to see the Body of Christ free from myths that have kept Christians in bondage for far too long. We believe that the Bible has answers, whether directly or indirectly, for every situation Christians may face. We use the Word of God and spiritual gifts to counsel people from all over the world, who face problems that they cannot take to others around them, and who are seeking answers they cannot find elsewhere.

Check out also our *Bible Issues* website (www.bibleissues.org) for Bible study topics and resources (great for personal and group Bible study) as well as our Facebook group (www.facebook.com/groups/bibleissues).

ALSO IN THE 8 MYTHS SERIES

A revelation of the bigness of God can set you free from a lot of things that create bondage in your life

You may download a FREE chapter at
www.8myths.com/free

FREE E-BOOK on Spiritual Warfare and the Armor of God

www.8myths.com/warfare

POST A REVIEW

We pray that this book has been a blessing to you. It will help us a long way if you posted a review. It does not have to be an elaborate review. If you have specific things to say, by all means do so. But reviews could also be very simple like, "Great book", "Highly recommended", "It has been a tremendous blessing to me." Even if you hated the book and you would like to put a negative review, even that is welcome.

You need to go to the same page where you purchased the book and post your review. You can use the link below to get to your review page. Thank you and may God continue to bless you and give you the desires of your heart.

www.8myths.com/review

Printed in Poland
by Amazon Fulfillment
Poland Sp. z o.o., Wrocław